BEAUTIFYING THE BODY

IN ANCIENT AFRICA AND TODAY

BEAUTIFYING THE BODY

IN ANCIENT AFRICA AND TODAY

CHRISTELLE KEDI

To my
sister SUAAD
beauty 2013
6th July
London
C. Kedi

WWW.BOOKSOFAFRICA.COM

Publisher:
Books of Africa Limited
16 Overhill Road
East Dulwich, London
SE22 0PH
United Kingdom
Web site: www.booksofafrica.com
Emails: admin@booksofafrica.com
sales@booksofafrica.com

ISBN: 978-0-9566380-6-9

A CIP catalogue record for this book is available from the British Library.

BEAUTIFYING THE BODY

IN ANCIENT AFRICA AND TODAY

CONTENTS

ACKNOWLEDGMENTS

I would like to thank our witnesses who accepted the long process of being interviewed and of delivering their "histories".

Thanks also to our editor, Nigel Watt, and publisher, Emmanuel Mah, for their incredible patience and professionalism. Without them this book may have taken a slightly different direction. I owe a debt to the beauty professionals for having allowed (or for leading) us to open the eyes on our culture and those of the people related to our continent of origin. I would like to make a sincere mention of Paul Asquith, Franck Dossa, Nathalie Montlouis, Pawel Szewczyk, Fatou Fatal and Crystal Deroche for their support throughout this process.

Christelle Kedi

Books of Africa is grateful to AFFORD for help in raising funds to enable this book to be published.

INTRODUCTION

Image in a mass consumer society is a something to be marketed and sold. Selling is the action of exchanging something for money. We buy what is offered to us, what we like, what seems to please us without necessarily feeling any need for it. Seeing, buying, consuming. Modern " westerners " tend to visualise the world in threes: seeing, buying and consuming. This "trinity" can be seen at all levels in the Western lifestyle: reading, writing and arithmetic; Father, Son and Holy Spirit; working, banking, owning property; people, things and places.

For Bantu speakers of Nubian[1] origin, the world is multi-dimensional. It is perceived as a demonstration of different elements of the "whole": mineral, water, fire, air, metal; physical, mental, spiritual, and sacred. Separated in three categories: physical (matter), esoteric (particles) and ethereal (pure energy), they have developed their conception of the world and aesthetics according to a relationship with the "whole". As in ancient Egypt, wearing masks is perceived as a "symbolic" connection with the

---

1. Nubians were the original inhabitants of the region along the Nile river, located in northern Sudan and southern Egypt. They were also known as Kush. By extension they were considered as the ancient Africans.

basic principles which create the different levels of energy or vibration. This Nubian way of seeing the world: perceiving (matter, basic particles and energy), experiencing (matter, basic particles and energy) and reasoning (matter, basic particles and energy) is possible only for those who are sensitive to different physical, mental and spiritual practices.

In both cases, the Nubian and Western lifestyles are necessarily the consequences of their own representation of things. Modern Western people put their trust only in physical experiences to understand the world; while the Nubians originally could experience the world fully only if they perceived it through different vibrations.

How could we therefore pretend that one of them could explain the other? How can Western societies who see the world in three dimensions understand that Nubian people communicated with spirits in various forms or with incense? How can we understand that westerners do not even get near to the aesthetic codes within Nubian creativity which are completely focused on the multidimensional representation of a world in constant vibration?

People descended originally from Africa (ancient Nubia) are estimated to number about one million eight hundred thousand in the UK[2], one of the largest "black" communities in Europe: a huge market. Big names in the cosmetics industry are well aware of the effects of cold on dark skins and know they require specific care to protect them from the effects of cold weather, lack of sun and hard water. According to Rob Walker[3], Black women in UK spent six times more on hair care products than their white counterparts[4] due to the many products used for the hair straightening chemical processes that we will explain later. These companies have in recent years developed a range of products to protect these dark skins from getting dry, pale and flaking off, typical effects of skin that has been badly cared for, promising that SPF 15 was one of the best components of beauty creams as it delays ageing of the

---

2. http://en.wikipedia.org/wiki/Black_British

3. Euromonitor International article on 14 September 2012 *Ethnic Beauty Care poised for a New Area of Growth*

4. L'Oréal study in 2005

skin. These multinationals have been quickly followed and caught up by thousands of small brands all claiming they are specialized in cosmetics adapted to dark or mixed-race skin and targeting the same market. Regarding products for Afro hair, an estimated four billion US dollars will be spent on them in 2013 alone[5]. Let us start this analysis by first looking at ancient Nubian beauty secrets with their links to this culture of body adornment. On our journey we will mainly focus on five main aspects: hair care, skin care the meaning of clothing, significance of colours and finally the body and head wrapping tradition – and the uses of these three within the aesthetics of ancient and contemporary African societies.

5. According to Joy Phido in her video *Business of Afro Hair* (2010)

PART I: AFRO HAIR

Studying Nubian aesthetics has followed several fundamental ways of understanding the mechanisms used to interpret these aesthetic codes. When studying Western fashion history, we are traditionally taught that individuals show their individuality through their styling and body adornment. We are even taught that fashion has a presence in every part of the socio-political life of every human society. This view refers to probably only one part of the history of body adornment and styling. It is certainly an authentic expression of one view of aesthetics but is only applicable to societies which are related geographically and culturally. It is true that among ideas based on studies related to human behaviour with regard to dress and adornment, the classical rule is based on three things: culture, partner and parent. The mother will be the first influence in the life of a young child: it is often she who will choose her hairstyle, her clothes and her skin care for many years. When the child grows up, the social context dictates his or her dress code and perception of beauty. An adult living with a spouse or partner will seem automatically to have been influenced by the partner's views. This works well when considering the idea of beauty in Western or westernized societies.

However, when observing "Africans" in all their diversity, we quickly realise that attitudes to beauty may still be an individual affirmation but are much more the footprint of a community. Ideally and initially, in every community, men and women looked alike! The best examples are among the Ptah[6] (also known as Pygmies) communities where, apart from the obvious difference of gender, men and women resembled each other. Among the Tuareg, all women look alike and all men look alike! No place for individual styling! A person only exists as an element of his culture and any influences from parents or partners are suppressed. Thus the only point at which European and "African" concepts meet is when celebrating the concept of "beauty" as a way of identifying a group. That is the reason why we have chosen to focus first on analyzing chronologically, spiritually and artistically the most widespread and obvious point of identification among Africans, their hair. 70% of Africans have frizzy hair, 30% have some kind of curly or wavy hair[7]. As we shall see in the following examples « Afro » hair showed that one belonged to a group. It was never a question of following the latest fashion.

1) THE NATURE OF AFRO HAIR

There are two types of human hair: the Indo-European and the African type of hair which can be divided into four categories which are again divided into sub-categories. The Indo-European straight hair is type 1. The hair known as "Mediterranean" is type 2. Types 3 and 4 are African hair. If African hair type is left uncut on a male subject it would reach a maximum length of between 55 and 70 cm while a woman's could expect to reach 88 cm to 1m depending on age and exposure to sunlight, both of which accelerate hair growth. On the basis of current canons of beauty, Asian people are the luckiest as their hair growth is the fastest, with a wide, round

---

6. Ptah were deities among the ancient Nubians from Abu Simbel and Gerf Hussein. They were known to be the forefathers of the first dynasties and of short height: http://en.wikipedia.org/wiki/Ptah

7. Encyclopaedia of Hair, a Cultural History by Victoria Sherrow. (Greenwood Publishing Group2006)

stem implanted 7mm inside the dermis, giving strong hair which grows fast. African hair type is flat and more or less rounded and forms various kinds of curls: wavy or frizzy with either fine or thick stems. The speed of growth is rarely faster than 1,5cm per month. Natural curl formation is linked to the process of cell division that occurs in the dermal papilla at the root of the hair: it is all based on genetics.[8]

With a stock of melanin cells available from birth, human hair is more likely to be black, brown or dark chestnut. Blond and red hair are characteristics of people who have a lack of melanin cells either through genes, as in the case of Scandinavian people and of negroid Albinos, or as a consequence of beauty practices aiming at creating blond hair. These techniques are often based on using plants, fruit or chemical compounds such as peroxide applied to the hair or by exposure to sunlight. Aristocrats in ancient Rome such as the Emperor Claudius, whose hair turned blond, and women in 15th to 17th century Portugal and Spain used to expose their hair (but not their skin) to the sun and to apply camomile mixed with water[9]. Once this solution has penetrated the roots of the hair where the melanin cells are found, it modifies the chemical structure of the melanin so that the hair, as soon as is exposed to the sun, gets fairer and fairer. The most striking example is among black populations of nomads of Somalia who until the 19th and early 20th century lightened their hair by applying lime juice before exposing their hair to the sun[10]. Because blond hair is naturally

8. *Afro hair, a Salon Handbook* by Philip Hatton (Blackwell Scientific 1994)

9. *Fashion in Hair* by Richard Corson (Peter Owen 1965)

10. Akou H.M *The Politics of Dress in Somali Culture*, (Indiana University Press 2011)

rare, it has fascinated dark haired people throughout history. Nowadays this phenomenon still exists with the culture of celebrities where "fashion icons" promoted by the media as examples of perfection are copied by their admirers. As Dr Nathalie Montlouis, a sociologist from Martinique, has explained in her thesis on 21st century violence against black women through the use of images[11], the "black woman" is a concept promoted by the mainstream media dominated by white men, money and "white" culture. It is easy to understand why some Barbadian celebrities have to try to please this audience which is their "market". To do this they would bleach or straighten their hair and conform to the public stereotypes of a black woman – half-naked and sexy.

Returning to the story of hair, it is in three parts, American, Caribbean and African as we mentioned at the start: we all know now that styling and body adornment in different human societies are the result of geographical and socio-cultural circumstances which affect the perception of beauty. When science tells us that the hair bulb determines the type of hair a person will have, how can we explain that so many "Nubian " women hope and dream of straightening their hair while genetically this is against their very own nature? The only explanation must be external influences and self-hate, whether conscious or not.

When we ask women who go in for hair straightening or wearing wigs to explain why are they so keen on adopting this quick option which may have unforeseen results, they will reply with one voice that straight hair is easier to manage. When asked how their grand mothers and ancestors used to style their hair before the straightening creams appeared they will give different answers according to their geographical and socio-cultural origins - what Dr Marimba Ani[12] called the "Asili"[13], the seed of culture. The African-American woman will tell you that these practices date from the time of the trans-Atlantic slave trade.

---

11. Available at the School of Oriental and African Studies, London

12. , Dr Donna Richards http://en.wikipedia.org/wiki/Marimba_Ani

13. Susan Hawthorne. *Wild politics: feminism, globalisation, bio/diversity.* Spinifex Press (2002). pp. 17–19

In this context a wonderful documentary book was published many years ago entitled "400 Years without a Comb", written by the historian Dr Willie L. Morrow. In his book, Dr Morrow explains the process of acculturation that the African-Americans experienced during their 400 years of slavery. Brutally cut off their geographical, cultural and social environment they were brought to America to work as slaves as a minority separated from each other. Most of the plantations in the south of the USA were not huge estates as we have been led to believe. A poor white American could exploit Irish and indigenous American labourers and African slaves. As the dominant ethnic group, the English-speaking Americans had a better knowledge of the land than any other non-indigenous group; they brought with them their cultures and ...combs. The isolation and distance from one plantation to another was so big that communicating among slaves was close to impossible so if they had little knowledge of basic hair care they had no means to ask about it. African-Americans at that time had little or no access to essential oils, avocado or "afro" combs. Dr Morrow's book focuses on the absence of Afro combs in US history over four centuries. As a consequence, the development of hair straightening techniques became the only socio-cultural and environmental solution to deal with Afro hair at that time.

West Indian hair has a different history. There were greater numbers of African slaves and the plantations were closer together, so they could communicate and exchange knowledge. Hair straightening was practised on a smaller scale and there were more mixed race people who were often born with loose curls or even straight hair, and because of the climate and natural resources found in the Caribbean they could experiment or reconstruct their hair care regime using the appropriate products (coconut oil, fruit, essential oils...). Straightening the hair was thus more the result of genetics: more people were "black" and the mixed-raced people were seen as a "racial solution" as is suggested by Frantz Fanon in his book, *Black skins, white masks* in which he explains the culture of straight hair, fair skin and aquiline nose celebrated by people in

Martinique as the only way to be "racially saved"[14]. The tradition of head-wrapping among women in the Caribbean should also be mentioned and will be explained on our last chapter.The masters of the plantations considered African hair not to be elegant and black women were obliged to hide their hair to avoid the offence of causing their hair falling onto the food served to the plantation owners. Head-wrapping was and still part of Caribbean culture as a response to the Nubian rules of body adornment.

The black people who remained in Africa and experienced colonization also have their own history of hair which is different from that of the African-Americans and African-Caribbean. The relationship between the Nubians and their hair is and has been uninterrupted since ancient times. The most long lasting hairstyling option in ancient Africa was hair braiding which included plaits, cornrows and box braids and was acceptable to the legal, political and social establishment[15]. Hair braiding was one of a number of cultural practices of non-verbal communication which were preserved wherever there was an African presence. We should start by understanding the structure of Nubian hair. Human hair is made of a cuticle, a cortex and a marrow or medullary area.

(Structure of hair. Microfinril /Microfibrilla, Macrofibril / Macrofibrilla, Cortex, Cuticule)

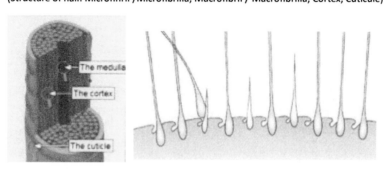

Cuticle: Outer protective layer made up of scales.

Cortex: Second layer of the hair giving 75% of its strength to the Afro hair.

Marrow also called the medullary area is invisible in thick hair

---

14. Slave women in Caribbean Society 1650-1838 by Barbara Bush (Heinemann, 1990)

15. *Natural Hair Care and Braiding* by Diane Carol Bailey (Milady 1998)

as it is deeply covered within the hair. Please note that people with very thin hair do not possess a marrow in their hair.

The renewal of cells on the scalp takes place over a cycle ranging from several weeks to several months. On a daily basis, the growth of hair varies from 0.23mm to 0.60mm per day that is between 0.7 and 2 cms per month. The life expectancy of Afro hair is between 4 and 7 years for women and 2 to 4 years for men if correctly groomed and maintained (with nourishment, sun, massage and care). In the classification of human hair the African variety is of types 3 and 4, which are divided into sub-categories 3a, 3b and 3c, also 4a and 4b.This type of hair grows superficially, at a depth of only 2.5mm. Its stem is oval and appears flattened and twists in spirals; it grows more slowly.According to Ginger Browne in her book, Afro Hair: procedures and techniques, Afro type hair can be divided into four different types: wiry hair (hard and glassy feel) often seen on mixed race people; coarse hair which is generally perceived as challenging to style; normal to medium hair which is the most common category and is half-way between coarse and fine hair; and fine hair which tends to be spongy as it lacks the medulla.

Hair type classification

Ethnicity	Pattern	Type	Color	Shaft
African	Curly/Kinky	3 & 4	Dark	Flat
Asian	Straight	1	Dark	Circular
Caucasian	Wavy/Straight	1&2	Light/Dark	Oval

Growth depends on gender, the origin and lifestyle of individuals and genes. However, it is possible to work out statistics of the percentages of the types of hair but it is challenging to classify each sub-category - wavy, frizzy, thick or thin stems - as hair may appear the same and behave differently. African type hair is able to absorb huge quantities of liquids, even more if the liquids are alkaline. The hair porosity is associated with the state of the cuticle. Because

African hair type tends to be more porous at its points, the use of steam treatment with dry heat or use of steam and excessive alkaline products such as hair strengtheners and bleaching products may increase its porosity and permanently damage it.[16]This absorption causes the fiber to swell due to the opening of the layers of the cuticle. The porosity test which every professional hairdresser of « African » hair uses is simple: it is a way of checking the condition of the hair to see the level and speed at which treatment is absorbed. Non porous hair means longer treatment time while porous hair means quicker absorption. Since porosity is never exactly the same over the whole scalp, a hairdresser will pull out a few strands of hair until they are straight then hold them near the tip of the hair and will then slide her fingers down the hair towards the roots. If the hair is soft it will be less porous but if it is abrasive it will be very porous.

Acids and alkalis with African hair type

0 1 2 3 4 5	6 7 8	9 10 11 12
Acid Ph value (conditioners)	Neutral	Alkaline Ph value (straightener)

When the hair has been moistened with water or an alkaline solution the keratin fibre swells and softens. The natural process of oxygenation ("a chemical process that involves combining a substance with oxygen" occurring in bleaching, permanent colour when neutralising a perm")[17] takes place when the hair is wet. The elasticity test is to verify the condition of the cortex.While keeping the fingers near the roots, pull them gently until the natural knots have been stretched to the maximum. Now observe how quickly the hair untangles and returns to its initial form. This test is more effective if the hair is wet. Hair that has lost its springiness is difficult to straighten or transform in any way. Hair only falls out two or three months after the death of the cells that produce it,

---

16. *Hairdressing Science* by Florence Openshaw (Longman 1982)
17. *Illustrated Hairdressing Dictionary* Hiscock (Pearson 2008)

spontaneously or pathologically though the time can be reduced by action such as combing, rubbing or shampooing the hair. Combs tend to stick on the crinkle and tear the cuticle causing the hair to break off at its ends due to uneven keratinisation during the growing phase of every hair.[18]

With a natural reserve of melanin from birth, the hair bulb determines the type of hair. Hair thus has its own life cycle and hormone control. For people of Nubian descent, the stock of hair at birth is between 100 000 and 150 000 strands which are 10 to 15% less than for those of Indo-European descent. Hair becomes white as the reserve of melanin diminishes but this process can be reversed by eating plenty of alkaline green vegetables. The numbers of such cases are frequent among peoples who favour uncooked or vegetarian food.

2) HISTORY OF NUBIAN HAIR CARE

Traditionally in ancient African cultures, thick, styled and preferably long hair was associated with health, respectability and fertility. On the other hand, scruffy hair was about mourning, illness or anti-social behaviour[19]. From time immemorial regardless of culture and gender Africans gave great importance to hair care and to those responsible for it. Hairstylists, hairdressers, wigmakers, specialists making head wrappers, hair extensions and hair dying were a respected profession. One of the most famous hairdressers was Inu who was at the court of the Pharaoh during the XIth Dynasty and whose mummy is in the Brooklyn Museum in New York. He is featured in Dr. Ashton's article about her research into the 5,000 year history of the African comb. At the time hairdressers were either paid a yearly allowance to work for a rich family to care for the hair of the females or males of the entire household. They were booked by appointment to be styled at home or outdoors. There were no special hairdressing saloons as hair care was considered part of body care in general and therefore was an

18. *Afro Hair - Procedures & Techniques* by Ginger Browne (Hyperion Books 1989)

19. *Natural Hair Care and Braiding* by Diane Carol Bailey (Milady 1998).

important social event where close friends met and could discuss the latest news. Yet it was above all a relatively personal matter: only selected individuals could have access to someone's hair. The earliest examples of hair braiding could be traced back to the city called Saqqara, burial site of pre-dynastic royals. The main picture (still available nowadays at the Brooklyn Museum in New York) shows the tomb of Akhethoptep in which a government official is braided (2,630-2,540 BCE). More recent braiding history in Africa is revealed on a sixth century vessel from modern Congo where an African woman has her hair braided[20]. As a non-verbal form of communication, hair braiding was never only for beauty purposes. Sources of information about gender, age, geography, social status, spirituality and occupation show that hair braiding is still a social marker as well as a trendy form of body adornment. Agriculture was central to the life of ancient Africans. Basic techniques of hair braiding were an artistic expression of agriculture[21]: hair braiding was an exercise during which the comb would replace the hoe used by farmers to part the hair on scalp. The action of fertilizing the soil was performed on human scalp when oil was applied to the head. Braiding hair was like cultivating the soil. Cornrows are typical examples of a braided hairstyle recalling the agricultural source inspiration.

Body adornment through temporary body modification includes techniques styling both the hair and the body which aim to identify, mark out and embellish the individual. These techniques are called "temporary" because their effects are limited in time from a few hours to a few months. These hair choices can be undone or changed. What we call temporary body adornment techniques include clothing, dyeing, hairstyling, hairdressing, make up and some tattooing and piercing methods. Body adornment comprises a number of methods of body modification which identify an individual within or outside his or her social group. Family, community, age group, faith and gender could each potentially

20. *Through African Eyes, Vol 1. The past: Road to Independence* by Leon E. Clark (CITE Books 1999)

21. *Natural hair care and braiding* by Diane Carol Bailey op.cit.

be indicated by a physical difference. Clothing, hairdressing and make up identified a person's personal history, social condition and economic status. Pierre Bourdieu in his 1980 book, *a Social Critique of the Judgment of Taste* shows that in highly organized or state-controlled societies individuals' bodies were subject to a number of social rules which categorized them according to social, economic, symbolic and hierarchic criteria. The most significant examples in the ancient pre-colonial cultures of the continent are the body modification techniques which carry a message.

Hairstyling is one of these as it shows the social status of a man or especially a woman. Wearing a wig in ancient pre-dynastic Egypt among the upper classes was perceived as a sign of wealth and material comfort. Males wearing wigs shaved from head to toe in order to avoid infestation by lice.

Up until approximately 1150 BCE, wigs were mainly designed to be made of dark colours. The massive arrival of communities of Indo-European origin led to the development of different colours and a wider use of wigs. It is interesting to note that pre-dynastic Egyptian societies were using wigs made mainly of vegetable fibre or sometimes of wool, rarely, human hair[22]; and towards the end of the dynastic period in Egypt, horse hair. By the time of the HyKsos[23] dynasties, the horse hair wigs in light colours were widely spread across the kingdom, a fact which also confirms that the demographics at the time had increasingly changed to a more multi-ethnic society. In all cases wigs were made on a small scale and of natural materials which allow the skin to breathe and the head to be aerated. Wax and plant fibres were mixed with a wool, horse hair or human hair making horizontal lines. Triangular wigs were common in pre-dynastic Egypt, but in the later period rectangular wigs were more common

Note that in ancient Rome, blond wigs were worn exclusively by courtesans and working prostitutes. Roman law demanded that these women distinguish themselves by their hair. Prostitutes who

---

22. *Fashion in Hair* by Richard Corson. (Peter Owen1965)

23. Also known in Greek as Hykussos (Υκουσσώς) between the XI and XIII dynasties, Indo-Europeans who ruled ancient Kemet.

had no wig had to dye their hair blond to show that they belonged to this profession. It is much later that the practice of wearing blond hair became a status symbol and a symbol of beauty among the upper classes and the law was changed. The new trend started when the third wife of the emperor Claudius used to wear a blond wig each time she went to a brothel, so as not to be recognised. Dido, the Queen of Carthage, was famous for her dark eyes and natural long blond hair which was still quite rare in North Africa in her day. Regular contact with Scandinavian people and the beginning of a new era in which the descendants of the Ottoman Turks had become rulers of the North African coast certainly influenced the aesthetic code and notions of beauty. Years later, after the fall of most of the ancient civilizations, blond hair became popular and remains to this day a primary beauty criterion in Western society.

Dr. Sally-Ann Ashton has written in her article introducing her exhibition of the 5,000 year history of the African comb[24] that the way in which the comb changed explains and bears witness to the ethnic variety and the demographics of the different eras of ancient Egypt. The combs found in tombs are exactly like those found in modern Africa, while in the Ptolemaic period a comb was produced with two sides, one "African" and one "European".

In his book published in 1602, the Dutch explorer Pieter de Marees gave details of the sixteen most common hairstyles which greatly impressed him when he visited the African "gold coast". Hairstyling and hairdressing focus on the head, the thinking organ, the highest point of the human body with its spiritual, aesthetic and social significance. Neglected hair, uncared for and dirty, would be associated with mourning, illness, anti-social or criminal behaviour. Hairstyles were very often temporary: prosperous Africans aimed to change their hairstyles daily. This involved washing, combing out, hydrating and finally styling. Fashionable styles were plaits, braids, locks, twists, knots, curls and cornrows... and styles were designed according to a woman's position and status in society -

24. Founder for the origins of Afro Comb exhibition http://www.originsoftheafrocomb. co.uk/combs/

widow, teenager, married or pregnant woman. Below are examples of methods of global identification of women by their hairstyles.[25]

Finally, regarding the process of shampooing: a mixture of water with the juices of many plants, including *aloe vera,* thyme and nettles was easiest and cheapest for most people. The use of saponins from the root of the carnation was much appreciated by people in ancient Egypt who used it as it created foam when mixed with water and was efficient in cleansing human skin and destroying body dirt. The Egyptians added animal fat and essential oils to the saponin to soften and add fragrance to a variety of

25. *Natural hair care and braiding* by Diane Carol Bailey (Milady 1998)

soaps. Sumerians found out that mixing water with cassia oil and alkanet would produce a skin cleanser. The ancient Romans had also noticed that the animal fat which dripped from the fire when cooking meat foamed when it encountered the water of the River Tiber and this spot where there were cinders and ash from cooking and clay soil by the river became a well-known place for washing.

Later on, it is interesting to note that African slaves who had been brought to the United States of America during the conquest of the west developed "dry shampoo" since access to water was extremely difficult, resulting in the "all body cleansing process". They used powdered corn (maize) which they mixed with fats and oils, using eggs for combing out. This mixture is very close to *Swabu*, a cleaning agent used in ancient Egypt derived from natron. A mixture of alkaline salts, animal fats and essential oils, it was effective for skin problems and for cleaning the epidermis. Some of these dry shampooing practices are still in use today. In some central and southern African countries fat is mixed with pawpaw (papaya) juice and ashes to make a cleaning soap[26].

Traditionally, Berber women from Morocco wash their hair using clay (*rassoul*) which comes in various colours depending on its mineral content. White clay or kaolin, has similar reactions on both skin and scalp. There are different types of clay which have the same cleansing and absorbing effects both for the skin and the scalp, internally and externally. Clay is a sedimentary deposit rich in mineral elements such as calcium, iron, magnesium, phosphorus, selenium, zinc, cobalt and manganese. It assists healing, cleansing and rejuvenating. It provides necessary mineral elements, is anti-inflammatory and antiseptic. It is an age old, natural remedy. The various kinds of clay, white, yellow, grey, red, green and pink, provide for the human skin's many different needs. Its high mineral content gives back life to lifeless hair. This table shows the properties of different clays:

---

26. *Fashion in Make- up from Ancient to Modern Times* by Robert Corson (Peter Owen 1972)

WHITE	OLIGO-ELE-MENTS	PROVIDES MINERAL ELE-MENTS AND CLEASNSES	REVITAL-ISES DRY AND LIELESS HAIR	SOFTENS AND CALMS
GREEN	VARIOUS MINERALS	REMOVES PIMPLES	REDUCES EXCESS OF SEBUM	REGENERATES AND DRIES
YELLOW	MANGANESE	STIMULATES PRODUCTION OF IRON AND COLLAGEN	REGENERATES CELLS	STIMULATES AND ADDS TONE
PINK	IRON AND MINERALS	ACTIVATES BLOOD CIRCU-LATION AND ADDS MINER-ALS	ADDS SHINE TO HAIR CO-LOURING	NOURISHES AND FORTIFIES
RED	IRON OXIDE AND OLIGO-ELEMENTS	REVIVES AND ACTIVATES CIRCULATION OF BLOOD	ADDS SPARKLE TO HAIR AND COLOURING	PURIFIES AND CLEANS

Formula for making a snow doll.

Ingredients: 6 tablespoons of kaolin, 3 tablespoons of virgin olive oil.

Mix all the ingredients in a glass bowl and apply the mixture on to a dry scalp which is ready to be washed. Leave it for at least 90 minutes, or at most for half a day (when the clay starts drying). Then rinse thoroughly in warm water and treat the hair with oil.

To cleanse and get the most of your natural Afro type hair, the best way is to shampoo your hair with eggs. Most modern shampoos sold today contain sulphate which is the element responsible for the intense foam and for making the scalp and African hair dry. Even using a conditioner does not necessarily alleviate these effects. Some opinions regarding natural hair would say that shampoos are not dangerous, so why are we getting all these hair issues while our grandmothers did not experience them? Below, find two options which could be used alternately: the cool option for the first week's wash and the clay option the following week. If your hair is type 4 always condition your hair with an oil bath before and after these cleansing processes.

1) Cool option: 2 teaspoons of honey, 1 egg (yolk only), 3 tablespoons of virgin almond oil.

Mix all the ingredients in a glass bowl and apply to dry hair which is ready to be washed. Leave the mixture on for at least 30 minutes and maximum one hour (once the egg is dry). Rinse thoroughly in warm water and apply your oil treatment.

2) **Clay option**: 5 tablespoons of white clay (kaolin) ; one egg yolk.

Keep the mixture for at least an hour and then rinse thoroughly with warm or cold water.

Hydration and Protection

Oil treatments are the ideal combination for hydration of hair types 3 & 4. Either you set up an oil treatment (shown above for types 3 and 4) and leave it on your hair for at least an hour with preferably a hot towel on your head to maximize the treatment or you add a half avocado to get a richer and more effective result. In that case you can only keep the mask for an hour maximum.

Almond mask (or Almond oil treatment): 1 tablespoon of ground almond powder, 1 bunch of thyme.

The handful of thyme should be boiled for 5 minutes in ½ litre of water. Leave the thyme mixture for 10 minutes to cool down then add to the others ingredients. Thoroughly mix the solution (thyme and water)with the ground almonds.

Shea butter mask: 1 tablespoon of avocado oil or ¾ of a smashed avocado, 3 tablespoons of shea butter, 1 tablespoon of wheat oil.

Once you have set up the recipes, you need to cut your hair into different small sections and apply the mixture gently so that it penetrates well into the hair and the scalp. Keep your hair warm by using a hot towel them for 30 to 45 minutes then rinse thoroughly with warm water. Note that gels were a common practice among ancient African cultures: the Yoruba mixed ochre with animal fat while the Malagasy mixed honey with animal fat.

Basic equipment for home-made cosmetics.

Glass bowls or containers, knives, earthenware containers, food mixers, fruit juicers, spoons, measuring equipment.

3) AFRO HAIR & COSMOGONY

The genealogy of Nimrod

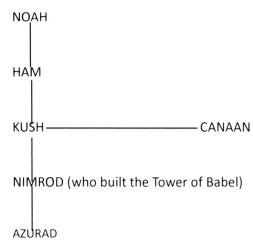

NOAH

HAM

KUSH ——————————————— CANAAN

NIMROD (who built the Tower of Babel)

AZURAD

a) Kemet and the Indo-Europeans: The spiritual foundation

As a way of identifying themselves, people of ancient Egypt of the dynastic periods (from 3,100 BCE) through their hair showed the link with the original Nubians, also known as *Ptah* or *Annunaki* by the Sumerians. These ancient Nubians[27] were perceived as the founders of the Kemet (also known as ancient Egyptian) civilization. The dark skin of a true Nubian made them believe that they were descended from both gods and men. Menes - or Narmer or Sarragon (his Sumerian name) or Nimrod (his Greek name) - was the last king of the ancient Kemet (or ancient Egyptian) pre-dynastic era and the first of the last 18 Egyptian dynasties and was a Nubian (or *Nuwaupu)* himself. He had dark skin and woolly hair and claimed this double origin, as a god and as a human being.

---

27. National Geographic (February 2008), Photographs of Nubian pharaohs by Kenneth Garrett

He claimed to be born from an *Annunaki* father, a god and from a human, Nubian mother from the Ptah community. According to the ancient Egyptian mythology, they believed that the first Nubian people had arrived from the star constellation Orion. Their preferred colour was green. In the Bible, he is the builder of the Tower of Babel. Their hair distinguished Nimrod and his people from those of the other important civilization of that period, the Hindu.

Hindus also had dark skins and their hair was black but straight. Hindus were known to identify themselves with their special number "six", their colour was "blue" and their preferred element is "water". Both Nubians and Hindus regarded hair as a "crown" given by the gods.

"Afro" hair type has particular characteristics essential for the synthesis of the sun's rays. It acts as a receptacle for this energy, thus allowing people in ancient Egypt to withstand the effects of the sun. It also transforms the sun's rays into vitamin D, a component which helps the body to assimilate calcium. The regulation of body temperature is also partly dependent on this type of hair. Nature (*neteru* in ancient Kemet) offers an alternative to melanin: it is called chlorophyll. Nubians (or *Nuwaupu)* considered themselves

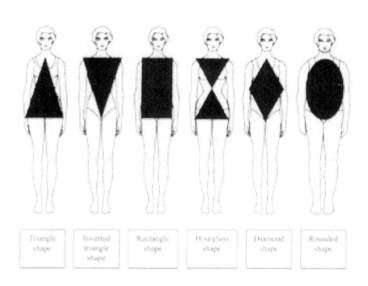

| Triangle shape | Inverted triangle shape | Rectangle shape | Hourglass shape | Diamond shape | Rounded shape |

to be a distinct people due to their physical differences: "afro" hair, broad nose, dark skin and "triangular" body type (see body shapes picture page 32).

b) Cosmology

In daily life, men and women used to wear wigs, masks, hats and headdresses (made of natural materials such as vegetable fibres). Their hair was their most treasured characteristic and a link with their ancestor "god", Annunaki. Women's hair was regarded as sacred and was cared for by using essential and vegetable oils. It was combed with the fingers or with combs with large teeth. Hair was carefully washed with spring water and, depending on the period, with black soap or essential oils. Women's hair was plaited or braided.

Frank Willett, the well-known archaeologist and art historian, explained in his 1993 re-edition of *African art: an Introduction* that the ancient Egyptian religion can only be better understood with reference to sub-Saharan African religions. In the same book he also adds that ancient Egypt had an African culture and that the pre-dynastic Egyptian art shows essentially African characteristics. According to him Egyptian statues played the same cultural role as modern African sculpture all over the continent. Characterized by a lack of facial expression and using symbolism, ancient Egyptian masks and statuettes underline the fact that "African" art has a spiritual function and is not only concerned with emotion or beauty which is a Western perception of art. African art is functional: the age of those portrayed in the statuettes is of no importance since their aim is to portray a deceased or well-loved person in a symbolic manner.

The process of creating art was highly sophisticated and ritualized: symbolism was the end product. What connection do we see today between the form of art in ancient Egypt and that of the Italian renaissance or of ancient Greece? We confirm again that the visions of beauty in Nubian and the Western societies were totally different. Nubian aesthetics are practical and can be appreciated by the whole community on a physical, mental and especially spiritual level.

4) HAIRSTYLING AND HAIRDRESSING

Today there is a fundamental difference between the professions of hairdresser and hairstylist. There are different levels of training. Hairdressers, beauty therapists, nail technicians and make-up artists have to graduate to a minimum of Level 3 which is equivalent to A levels. HABIA (the Hair and Beauty Industry Authority) has developed National Occupational Standards (NOS) as the basis of training in hair, beauty, nails and spa. They form the backbone of programmes such as National Vocational Qualifications, apprenticeships and codes of practice: hairdressers need to have reached level 3 to be able to join the Hairdressing Council created by the UK government in 1964 which acts similarly to the Law Society for the legal industry.[28]

To provide care and treatment for hair, only fully qualified hairdressers have the ability legally to supervise and deliver some chemical practices such as colouring or even cutting hair (i.e. a medium to long term effect on people's hair). Hairstylists (such as lockticians or braiders without a full level 3 in hairdressing) do not cut or dye hair or apply chemical products. They are hair artists, shaping the hair – and they are not necessarily formally trained for this work. This is the case with those who specialise in locks. Wig making, however, is a profession on the border between hairdressing and make-up, and for this a qualification is needed[29]. In the first case some countries and schools provide diplomas, though there is no harmonisation of the level of the qualifications; in the second case insurance for the work is dependent on a standard diploma issued by a professional body. University courses are even provided in some countries.

Hair care for types 1 and 2 (Indo-European) is easier as their scalp or rather the sebacious glands in the scalp continuously produce enough oil to hydrate the hair on a daily basis. This is why, for them, dandruff is a sign that too much oil or fat is being produced. One of the most effective ways of combating dandruff is to use shampoo once or twice a week.

---

28. Source: www.habia.org

29. National Occupational Standards (NOS)

For Afro hair type 3 and 4, the lack of oils, normally produced by the glands in the scalp, and the naturally curvy bulb of the hair, do not allow the natural moisturizing of the hair. Daily manual hydration and moisturizing is therefore needed. One of the features of having Afro hair is that because it is so dry it does not get dirty as quickly as in the case of types 1 and 2. And shamppoing using a "detergent" is only necessary two to three times a month but a daily application of oil, massaging it onto the hair and scalp, is essential. Note that treatment of the scalp is different from the extra care given to the hair itself.

On the African continent today 75% of people have (frizzy) hair type 4, 15% have (curly)type 3 and only 10% have (wavy) hair of type 2. Type 1 hair is found mainly among the Indo-European communities (Caucasians, Asians and Native Americans). Climate is a determining factor affecting hair type: in Africa today people living in a humid environment will have heavier and straighter hair while those living in drier areas will have lighter, more cylindrical hair to withstand the sun. A three month action plan is an efficient means of controlling hair growth. The real benefits can be seen with a winning and effective strategy over a minimum period of twelve months. Ideally this 12 month cycle can be divided into mini-cycles of 12 weeks during which the changes become visible and special care is needed when choosing care products depending on the season. When living in a temperate climate, adapting your hair regime to the cold months is vital. This could be compared to your food diet: eating the same vegetables every day for years might create some food deficiencies. To get the best results change your hair regime and products every three months, so as to stimulate and hydrate the hair. As hair tends to fall out two to three months after the spontaneous or pathological death of the cells from which it grows, this time can be reduced by friction and excessive cleansing using shampoos.

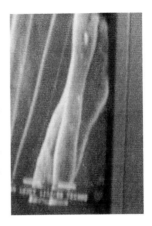

Hair of type 3a (curly) needs regular moisturizing of the scalp preferably with a dry oil and hydration of the hair with mineral water mixed with softening essential oils. Argan oil or olive oil or aloe vera can help the curls to become frizzy (type 3). This hair still needs to be protected from cold, from limestone in the water and from getting too dry. Well cared for hair and scalp allow hair to grow with a regular and visible rhythm. Curly hair of type 3b needs deeper hydration of the scalp with more stable dry oil such as coconut or Monoi. Alternatively, mineral water can be used to hydrate the hair alternating with essential oils or a mixture of dry oils. Watch your ends as the type of protection you choose and which suits the nature of your hair will determine the speed of growth: the more you style in a way which protects the hair, the ends and the pH[30], the better your chances of seeing your head of hair growing thicker, longer and more lovely. Type 3c (frizzy) needs weekly oil treatment as well as the special care recommended for type 3. Remember that the beauty of hair is measured not only by its length but by the ease with which it can be combed, its softness and the perfection of the curls. All types of frizzy hair when it is in good condition are capable of forming natural curls. Bad beauty habits or inappropriate care food result in split ends dry or broken "unmanageable Afro hair" - nothing else!

Hair type 4a is very frizzy and needs hydration of the scalp with a denser oil such as shea butter or castor oil. The scalp needs to be moisturized too. Usually, it is recommended to use a mixture of water and dry oil and shea butter or avocado oil. Type 4b is a softer frizzy hair requiring deep hydration of the scalp with castor oil (ricin) or avocado oil mixed with shea butter. The hair should for preference be hydrated with mineral water mixed with some essential oils. Type 4 is the driest of human hair. It needs weekly oil treatment and becomes very fragile when exposed to cold and it splits if not cared for. Care needs to routine and almost automatic. It loves water and rich food - nutrients such as vegetable protein, amino-acids and fruit. Growth is the slowest but

---

30. The pH scale measures how acidic or basic a substance is

the most spectacular when all the ingredients need to stimulate it are present!

a) Shaving the beard

According to Nicole Tyrimou, an analyst in beauty and personal care for *Euromonitor International*[31], men's skin care has advanced considerably. Economic changes leading to rising unemployment have influenced men to care more about their looks. According to *Euromonitor International*'s Annual Study related to young men's behaviour towards health and wellness, over a third of men are dieting! The fact that more men have been eating junk food has a negative effect on their skin leading them to buy more beauty products to enhance their features. In the past, bad habits affected their skins men looked for beauty "cures". Men's skin care products were thus the most sought-after category within the global beauty industry in 2011.

Shaving is a profession that dates from prehistoric times[32]. (The word "barber" originally referred to the beard but has become a general term for a men's hairdresser in modern times). Archaeologists have found blades, sharpened bones and flints used for shaving dating from as early as 30,000 years BCE. People of ancient Egypt were among the first to develop shaving as part of a daily routine. Bronze tools have been found in the tombs of the pharaohs of some dynasties dating back to over 6000 BCE. The word 'beard' comes from the Latin word 'barba' (French *la barbe*) which describes the facial hair on men surrounding the mouth and often developing on cheeks. The beard in ancient and some contemporary cultures symbolises strength, wisdom and virility. According to Maurice Lister in his book, *Men's Hairdressing: Traditional and Modern Barbering*, skilled and professionally trained barbers in ancient Egypt (1,500 BCE) were offering their services in the open air due to the dry climate. Barbers found their

---

31. "Men's Grooming on the Cusp of Transformation" article by Nicole Tyrimou published on 29 th October 2012 in Euromonitor International

32. *Men's Hairdressing: Traditional and Modern Barbering* by Maurice Lister (Thomson 2004)

customers outside in the street and they shaved them and cut their hair in the shade of a tree, visible to all. This is still the case today in Africa and other hot areas.

In ancient Hellenic times, Alexander the Great gave his soldiers new rules to stop his enemies grabbing Greek warriors by their beards on the battlefield. His later victories meant that the trend of shaving both hair and beard spread to the newly conquered lands and Alexander became a fashion icon of his time. In ancient Rome by 300 BCE, barbers were a highly respected and prosperous professional body. Barber shops were places where men would meet to discuss and share the latest news and gossip. This was a privilege of the richer classes, however. Men of lower class and slaves had to keep their hair and beard long to indicate their status.

The red and white barber's pole (red, white and blue in the United States) can be traced back to the Middle Ages when barbers also performed minor surgery such as pulling teeth, as well as haircutting and shaving. They were powerful and popular up until the Enlightenment in the 18th century. In Britain the roles of barber and surgeon were legally separated in the time of King George II in 1745.

b) A few tips before choosing a hairstyle

Considering a new head to confirm a new look requires some careful thought. Choosing a haircut and hairstyle is supposed to make you more photogenic. Changing your hairstyle changes, braiding your curls with cotton knots or deciding how long to grow your hair – all these are matters of taste, of how you want your face to look. Piling your hair high or making it voluminous has the effect of elongating your face especially if your face is round, e.g. Macy Gray while fringes are advantageous for angular faces, e.g. Oprah Winfrey or prominent foreheads, e.g. Sonia Rolland (Miss France 2000).

Hair tied back is ideal for those with oval faces and a small chin such as Queen Latifah or Liya Kebede. Short hair is best for those with ears very close to the head and perfectly symmetrical faces such as Alek Wek and Missy Elliott. Please do keep in mind your hair type to avoid any styling mistake. For example having thin hair makes it hard to get an Afro out of it. With unruly hair and a square face an Afro would make you look like a standard lamp.

Tinting your hair is only useful if you are planning to distract people from looking at your face. The singer Gabrielle did this to draw attention away from her eye-patch, as did Beyoncé because her eyes are asymmetrical. Finally your age, means and lifestyle will seriously affect your choice: a sportswoman or a female mechanic would think twice before growing her hair long – while a professional model might prefer to do so.

PART II: SKIN CARE

1) WHAT DOES « BLACK» SKIN REPRESENT?

a) Black skin, white Afro-cosmetics: analysing ethno-cosmetic marketing - the US example

The marketing strategies targeting black women consumers are numerous. They are all based on controlled and verifiable data: the place or country, perception, time, price and product can be adapted from one market to another. To analyse this phenomenon, we need to look briefly at the relationship an expatriate black woman can have with the cosmetics industry.

In her remarkable book dedicated to the "Afro-American" woman and her report on the economics of the beauty industry between 1920 and 1975, Susannah Walker describes how the birth of "ethno-cosmetics" as a marketing strategy greatly affected the relationship between black women consumers and the "world of beauty". The black US beauty market was created in the 1920s by the first women millionaires, "Madame" C.J. Walker and Annie Minerva Turnbo Pope Malone. These two ladies were among the first generation of African-Americans born free (in 1867 and 1869 respectively) soon after the Civil War[33]. They both quickly understood that the big US beauty industries looked down at black people and never considered them as a market for luxury beauty products because the industrialists saw blacks as ugly, poor and uncivilised. These pioneers also perceived the social and identity-creating aspect of black women's relationship with their bodies after centuries of oppression and dispossession. Only black people relate personal - not to say intimate - subjects such as hygiene and personal appearance to their communities. The need to rebuild first an individual identity and then a community required introspective therapy: a journey through the rediscovery of being a free black woman. Ethno-cosmetics were born. Despite the type of beauty products in vogue at the time: skin bleaching creams and hair straightening products, some black people built some of the most significant financial empires in the early 20th century in the USA[34]. It should be added that at the end of the 1920s big American cosmetics companies began to take an interest in these "ethnic" consumers and set up the Apex College of Beauty Culture in New York with compulsory options dedicated to cosmetic applications on dark skins, even while the racial segregation was still in force.

The 1930s were a definitive turning point in the black beauty industry in the USA in terms of the marketing strategy aimed at the "African- American" woman. The same products were available from both black and mainstream cosmetics producers. The only differences were over advertising strategies. For the cosmetics giants these were the same as those aimed at Caucasian women consumers: eternal beauty, health, charm and luxury. The black beauty moguls focused on the fact that they personally were also using the products they were selling. At the time of a massive migration to the cities from the countryside, the beauty cult was one of the few supra-racial data common among all US citizens. Luxury and premium offers were born!

33. Bundles, A'Lelia , *Madam C. J. Walker: Entrepreneur* (Chelsea House/Facts on File, 2008)

34. Bundles, A'Lelia *On Her Own Ground: The Life and Times of Madam C.J. Walker* (Lisa Drew Books/Scribner, 2001)

Until the late 1960s when racial segregation ended in the US, black women were submitted to mainstream beauty criteria due to their lack of visibility in the media and in society as well their own identity crisis. This made them want to appear as non-"Nubian" as possible by getting fairer skin and the straightest possible hair. These beauty stereotypes were also imposed on the other ethnic minority groups such as the Native Americans, Chinese and Puerto Rican Hispanics.

The 1970s transformed the image of the Nubian woman in the international context leaving behind the image of the slave or victim of colonialism to attain stardom in the cinema, music and the arts, in the intellectual field and in politics. Afro-cosmetics were born. The traditional "Bantu" hairstyles of Miriam Makeba, Rita Marley or Angela Davis led the way. Based on the use of natural beauty products imported from Africa and the Caribbean, Afro-cosmetics could promise black American women perpetual beauty and body hygiene!

The Masai, Bororos or Bambaras had beautiful hair and skins because they were close to their identity roots and therefore were using ancient natural beauty secrets.

Nowadays, black women living outside of Africa and the Caribbean tend to get lost in this confusing environment where beauty is commercialized and where there is a conflict between market research and the individual's self-image. Should this be natural, traditional or sophisticated? Straightened or curled?

This is how Europeans, Japanese, Chinese or white Brazilians gained a big part of the lucrative black beauty business, an industry where the law imposes very few checks and medical tests. Who has not heard of the "ethnic beauty shops" in Peckham and Brixton in south London, Harlem in New York or Château Rouge in Paris? All of them offer a wide range of products including locking product range for dreadlocks, skin bleaching creams and soaps, hair straightening products, all types of shampoo, face cream - probably with no information on the label. Their composition and origin is often unknown and they flow from America, Europe and

Asia into Africa, a "triangular trade" in reverse but still exploiting black people.

Made of hydroquinone and caustic soda which are normally only available through a prescription from a dermatologist, these products have become the most sought after by black men and women with the lowest income and educational level. There is no proper advertising on mainstream radio or television, there are no qualified beauty consultants to advise customers, no contra-indication, just an unscrupulous distribution network concerned more with profit than with customer care. The targeted market is made up of immigrants who are challenged socially, economically and in their own self-perception, people who may aspire to look brown rather than black, to have curls rather than frizzy hair.

Naomi Simms was created in 1986, Fashion Fair back in 1936 and both have developed a range of beauty products which have been dermatologically tested at least twice during their formulation process, once for accreditation for the US market and again for the European market. These products tend to attract more conscious consumers, socially established with self-confidence in their identity that have used similar products before and are trying to find the best care for their skin. These consumers, who are mostly women, also want to identify with a modern, westernized social context. They are generally from the southern hemisphere, especially Africa. They are proud of who they are and what they have achieved. Consciously or not, they would like to make the most of their natural attributes by caring for them and beautifying them.

Big companies such as Johnson and Johnson, l'Oréal, Procter and Gamble and Unilever have already shared the African market and have started to tap into its huge potential. Ivory Coast alone would generate approximately US $40 million according to an official study by the US federal Department of Commerce, which also suggests a one billion US dollar potential for South Africa and annual growth over the entire African continent of 25-35%. Another big cake to share!

The agreed expansion strategy for marketing on the continent would be to initiate consumers with low incomes to nicely packaged manufactured products as sold in luxury department stores. The social and professional elite would purchase more since this greater availability would mean that they could buy new products as soon as they arrive. In addition, given the large scale of the global cosmetics industry, governments with an eye to economic development are likely to look favorably on these beauty markets which would eventually create jobs for beauty consultants, beauticians and sales representatives.

What is the view of the companies concerned? Reality is different. The cosmetics industry is one where illusion is stronger than reality. The price of these "premium" products and the fact that they are manufactured outside Africa give them extra value in the eyes of African women. Thus, developing a local chain of production and local brands is still perceived as a commercial and strategic risk. Consumers might not be interested in buying beauty creams "made in Sierra Leone". The arrival of this massive beauty industry and the marketing that goes with it may, however, lead to a greater consciousness among African women. Being sought after as a consumer and cared for as a buyer will increase the self-esteem and confidence of African women and they may challenge this imported value system.

Who are we? Clients, consumers, beneficiaries...or are we all three? The UK Chartered Institute of Marketing has defined the marketing as managing the process of identifying, anticipating and satisfying the clients' demands in terms of profitability. In other words exchanging or offering services or products guaranteed to satisfy a need, calculated according to monetary value with no price limitations. This short definition transforms the consumer into a client-beneficiary. The identification of a product and its market is called marketing. A well planned strategy based on studying a targeted market generates demand from the category of consumers chosen. This is true of every product sold internationally and it would be interesting to go into more detail and see how marketing is affected not only by the consumer's perceived needs but on the availability of products in a given season or year and by the fact that, since they have a short life, consumers have to keep buying them regularly. Trade in cosmetics i.e. all substances used to enhance or protect the appearance and the odour of the human skin is worth US $330 billion worldwide (and US $18 billion in the US alone in 2007) according to a 2010 Harvard Business School report. With L'Oréal-Nestlé holding about 53% of the world market, can we say that this industry is only for multinationals?

The basis of modern marketing is the four 'p's: product, price, place and promotion, to which has been added, perception. From these fundamentals, a marketing strategy has to be defined for each product in order to reach specific objectives through market research and choice of method. How can this be done? By creating a strategy for each 'p'. Each strategy has to be carefully managed and must satisfy the needs of the consumer group that has already been identified. If you find the right commercial language, success is guaranteed!

For example, the promoters of "X Make-Up" would target black women in France aged 18-50 with a monthly income of around 1,400 euros (US $1,800). This product aims at selling a product designed for dark skins in a country where this same giant worldwide company founded in 1909 never really investigated this original "black"market in its own country, preferring to target the US black market! On the basis of this research, a premium price reflecting the luxury and exclusivity of the product would be charged. The product would only be sold in outlets such as department stores which would confirm its prestige. It would be promoted with an advertisement showing the first internationally famous black model contracted by US mainstream modeling agencies in the 1970s. This lady of "Nubian" origin was at the time starting a career in business and was to give her name to the new brand of make-up. In the UK, this brand is sold both in department stores and « ethnic shops" in areas where the black population is numerous, but it encounters the competition of US make-up brands already widely available in the UK.

Cosmetics marketing is a gold mine! In the case study mentioned, the product is perceived as different because the way in which this perception is created is based on the consumer's own motivation. How can we explain how in a market bombarded with new brands almost every week a multinational could completely neglect a class of consumer who really wants to spend money regardless of tax? It was nothing new, but displaying this black top model was enough to launch the brand in France. The public had no difficulty in identifying this beauty icon from the 70s, a symbol of a liberated African woman of the time, freed from her original beauty culture and embracing a new modeling career in the Big Apple - but she never forgot where she came from. She chose to give back to her community by adapting a Western vision of make-up colours, only suitable for Caucasian skins, for the worldwide community of African descent. This unique selling point is enough to motivate the female consumers to aspire to be that East African model and identify with her expatriation journey into the Western world.

The consumer's motivation is what creates need. At first there is a real need which constant media hype tends to eliminate. However, a moment always comes when the consumer is receptive or the competitors are asleep – and the consumer must feel herself to be unique. This is when the story of the famous first model to make an impression in this exclusive context helps to create the motivation to consume this range of products. Her unique selling point is exclusivity.

b) Nubian aesthetics and modern Western culture

Modern Western culture has created its own aesthetics and attitude to beauty resulting from the conditions in which the original people inhabiting northern lands evolved. Clothes, for example, protect you from the cold, indicate your profession, social status, gender and age, the latter being the least important. This is how the fashion industry and those professions linked to the creation of an image tend to respond to socio-historical and climatic reference points, influencing the consumer's sub-conscious.

In modern Western societies, men's and women's age has often to be concealed; gender is "neutralized", social status has to be subtly perceived, professions not boasted about and cold must be controlled. In such conditions the Scandinavian idea of beauty could easily fit: few in number and living in the coldest climates in Europe, they are a reminder of the legends and values of the Vikings. Always searching for new territories to conquer, the ancient Scandinavians were tall, pale, blue-eyed, fit, able to adapt to long days of darkness and long days with little night, to long distances on foot, to the cold... He is the opposite of the southerner, the *Ptah* (Pygmy), the mesomorphic body type, small, dark-skinned with woolly hair who evolved in equatorial climates where nature is generous and there is plenty of fruit to eat. He respects the ageing process because, as with nature, he becomes more mature and blossoms as he grows older.

The relative disappearance of the differences between men and women in modern Western cultures has resulted in aesthetic and cultural practices related to the idea of beauty. The misogyny latent in pre-Christian Europe has had consequences which continue into modern times: the idea of the woman being the weaker element, the "second sex", and weakness incarnate. Beauty in European art incites emotion. Renaissance art, like that of ancient Greece portrays women as full and rounded and men as heavy and muscular. The perfection of the human body was revealed despite the attitudes of what was already a materialistic Judeo-Christian society.

Nubian culture in the time of ancient Egypt was characterized by an obsession with cleanliness and status. Age, gender, profession, ethnicity, power and religion laid down a dress code during the pre-dynastic period. The Ptah considered themselves to be people with pure genetic traits. Today the unchanging physical appearance of these people is still a fact. A Khoisan[35] man does not look like a

---

35. **Khoisan** is a name given to two ethnic groups located in Southern Africa, sharing physical and linguistic similarities and not related to the Bantu majority in the area.

Baka[36] but they are more likely to resemble each other than they are with a Nilo-Saharian and a Bantu-speaker. Because of these similarities in appearance the only way to distinguish a man from a woman or a child from an adult was through dress, and this is still the case today among many of the oldest-established people of the continent. Clothing had – and has still for those who follow their ancestral religious practices – spiritual and ethereal as well as physical significance. Among the people of ancient Egypt only the upper classes were fully clothed! One fabric was dedicated to each human dimension: silk for the spirit, cotton for the soul, linen for what is ethereal and wool for the body. In ancient Egypt wool sometimes venerated and at other times disparaged due to its animal origin: rich people almost only wore cloth of plant origin whereas the poorer social classes wore little. African textiles tell us much about history, social distinctions and spirituality.

c) History of skin care in pre-colonial Nubian societies

Today, one of our main concerns is to be able to keep our make-up as long and fresh as possible whatever the climate. Durable make up techniques are no longer the privilege of film stars. By make-up we mean the practice using anything other than water, vegetables or fruit to beautify the human skin. What started as simple skin care has developed into cosmetics. Can we truly apply this term to the aesthetics of ancient Egypt?

Cosmetology is the science behind the making of skin care and beauty products which do not necessarily penetrate the seven layers of the dermis. There are three major types of human skin: bronze, beige and ivory. We will mainly focus here on the beige and bronze skins which characterize people with "Nubian" characteristics.

We should remember that when studying African aesthetics, the objects and ornaments associated with dress or body adornment are of two types: processes which modify the body and processes to embellish it. In the following examples, we will mainly focus on

---

36. **Baka** or **Baká** are an ethnic group similar to the Twa or Pygmies and living in the Republic of Congo, Central African Republic, Cameroon and Gabon

the body modification processes which can also be divided into two sub-categories: capillary (hair) and epidermic (skin).

Like geographers working drawing a new map, ancient African artists worked on a body of rules to develop techniques of long term body adornment. Treating the skin by modifying it permanently is one of a number of practices developed in different regions. African artists used oils, objects, plants and symbols originating from the areas where they worked. One of the best examples of the art of body modification can be seen on the Benin bronze statues (some of which can be seen in the British Museum) from 13th-17th century Nigeria. The warriors wore facial scars to identify their culture, gender and status.

Works of art represent people in their daily activities and adornment: clothes, cosmetics, hairstyle and status symbols. If we look closely at the statutes, sarcophagi and papyruses which have survived from ancient Egypt, we can certainly see that the artists have portrayed the dead in their eternal youth with black hair, youthful bodies, flawless skins, faces impeccably made up,: no wrinkles, spots, stretch marks, scars or veins. Obsessed with eternal life which followed physical death; the embalmers had a huge responsibility and were respected as a profession. Making a splendid sarcophagus and beautifully embalming the body were expensive rituals which earned spiritual veneration. Dressing up for the final journey involved all the techniques of long term adornment, creating a certain perception of reality: embellished, elevated and eternal. By marking forever the deceased with such adornment, the artist was at the same time excluding those who did not share his perception of beauty.

In the world of fashion, criteria of beauty are openly political by their very nature. By confirming what "beauty is" they define what is acceptable and what is not. From ancient times masculine youth has been considered an attribute of beauty. Taken together with health and with life as a whole, youth can be seen as a characteristic of beauty worldwide. The cult of appearance is scientifically accepted as an affirmation of a person's identity and personality.

d) Origin and use of Western cosmetics

In Western societies, removal of body hair (by waxing) became popular from the 1930s when swimwear was introduced as a popular product. During the 1960s, the popularity of mini-skirts encouraged women to follow this practice throughout the year. In the Middle East and Eastern Europe, these practices were already well known for centuries, probably due to the extreme or dry climates. In the ancient text of the "Hearst Papyrus"[37], the authentic guide to ancient Egypt's beauty and medical secrets, we can find recipes for anti-perspirant perfumes or waxing methods of hair removal for women and for priests. Waxed women were perceived as refined as they had removed their masculinity. Upper class people used to remove all forms of hair, including hair on the head where they wore wigs or other headgear.

The upper classes in pre-dynastic Egypt despised body hair which they associated with cave dwellers. Priests also had to remove all hair to be considered pure. Waxing using lemon, sugar and essential oils were the most common methods used.

It is important to remember that regular and rigorous skin hygiene is necessary if make-up is to last. If the skin could be compared to a wall where we want to paste wall paper, if the wall is not prepared even high quality paper will not stick. This is equally true for skin. Quality cosmetics require a basic skin care regime of cleansing, toning and moisturizing. The toning removes any remaining dust that the cleanser could not reach and closes the pores to prepare the skin to receive the moisturizer. All these steps are compulsory for the best results!

It strongly advised to use the same facial products on the neck for the simple reason that the neck is just as much exposed as the face and can show signs of age prematurely. Finally, your skin care regime must be adapted to your skin type: normal, oily, dry, mature or sensitive.

For people in ancient Egypt, myrrh was preferred for facial skin care as it leaves a pleasant scent, keeps the breath fresh and

---

37. Also known as the Hearst Medical Papyrus

disinfects the body. Myrrh was also used to refresh clothes, as a softener. Honey masks were used in the evening to give the facial skin deep moisturization and quick cell regeneration during the night.

Blushers aim to give colour to the face by applying it on the cheeks. It comes in the form of cream, powder, liquid or gel, and the most appropriate colours are the ones which go well with your skin tone and match your lip colour. For combination or oily skins, powder would be the best option. The lip liner was a major breakthrough for make-up in the 20th Century. These days it is still used regularly but has to be worn discretely with a neutral colour matching and never darker than your lips. Applying lip liner starts always in the middle of your natural lip line heading to the outer edges. If you need to readjust your lip liner put it in the refrigerator for up to 15 minutes (to solidify and process it). Choosing the right colour for your lips is priority as you will have to live with any mistake for six months or more and your taste might change... This precaution is important: imagine that you are walking in the street with your lips badly made up.

The lip liner must be applied along the natural line of your lips. It is best to start with the upper lip going towards the front of your mouth. If you need to sharpen your lip liner we suggest putting it first in the refrigerator for ten minutes to harden it. Careful choice of lipstick and a gloss is vital because these are long term investments compared to other cosmetics.

Those of us who have full lips will prefer bronze, violet and brown to balance the upper and lower parts of the face. Keeping the reds and bright colours for evenings out and always matching all of them with blushers and glosses. Red and pink tend to be the colours to use in rainy or cold weathers while peach, beige and terracotta are suitable for make-up in summer or in dry weather. In ancient Egypt red ochre and chalk mixed with dried red wine were used to make blusher, nail varnish or red lip colouring. Applying make-up in ancient Egypt was an art. Agility and perfect technique was required as the raw products contained a strong concentration of pigments. Cloves, copper sulphate, alum and olive oil mixed together in equal proportion would give a gentle paste causing less irritation than pure khôl. Some pigments extracted from other natural elements could be added to modify the colour such as green malachite (called *udju* by the ancient Egyptians) and antimony sulphide (which they called *mesdemet*); also saffron which was used as yellow eye shadow but was rare, expensive and in great demand for its authenticity. Jasper was another sought after beauty product for eye make-up with medicinal, beautifying qualities and popular with the court ladies as it was needed to keep the eye socket white. Burnt almonds were used to line the eyebrows and make the khôl last longer. Men only wore khôl under their eyes.

The eyelids would need to have a layer of foundation topped with some loose powder before initiating the application of eye shadow, eyeliner, mascara or pencil...This will allow the colour to last without creasing. There are special cosmetics such as eye primer or base which provide a guarantee in all conditions. It is normally used by make-up specialists but a very useful to ensure the make-up lasts through the night. To apply it, you need to moisturize your eye prior to it. If you want to use it you must apply this basis for the eyes: after applying hydrating cream and before applying background colour, pat the product lightly on your eyelid so that it does not get mixed with your hydrating cream. All make-up products should ideally be waterproof.

In ancient Egypt payments were often made in the form of beauty products. Milk baths were sought after by aristocrats who had large land holdings from which they could produce a reserve of fresh animal milk – including lion's milk! Honey was used in the embalmment or mummification process as it kept liquids within the body and could be used for face, hair or skin.

Eye shadow gives the eyes depth. Whether you use liquid, eye pencils or powder, it is always recommended to use two or three colours or tints to intensify the shadow. In all cases, the application should be performed with the help of a special eye shadow brush.

The most stylish colours to blend on brown eyes are green, bronze, champagne and chocolate brown. For darker eyes, we could keep the same colour range but add lime, turquoise and bright pink. Often without make-up but well shaved, eyebrows can be as important as any aspect of eye make-up. Their shape should remain the main focus. First bush your eyebrows and smooth with your fingers. The, using an eye pencil of the colour closest to that of your eyebrows can cover for any unevenness in the eyebrows, or for best results, invest in an eye shadow powder - sometimes also called eyebrow powder!

Khôl is a mixture, black or grey in colour, of galena or malachite with sulphur and animal fat, used by the ancient Egyptians for its medical, spiritual and beautifying effects. Its effect was frame the eyes in black, like cats' eyes or the frightened stare of the eternal child. "Cat eyes" make-up look was used to treat sinusitis, ocular irritation and eye strain due to sunlight. It had the effect of sunglasses for the Pharaohs and for people living in the desert. It can be mixed with other ingredients as required.

Eye make-up was common for both men and women as it had both spiritual symbolism and physical protection against redness caused by desert dust and sand. Large eyes were important for the people's idea of beauty. The Eye of Horus was the most familiar icon for amulets and for the design of eye make-up. Many ancient Greek historians referred to the obsession that ancient Egyptians had with their eyes, especially among the dynastic families.

Today, it is highly recommended to know about a skin type before choosing any skin product. Several options are available. The first is to visit a dermatologist for scientific and medical advice; the second option would be to go to beauty professionals such as beauticians, skin care advisors and make-up artists; or, the third and least effective option, finally to use your own judgment based on the handkerchief test: when you wake up in the morning, take a 100% cotton handkerchief, preferably white, and place it for five minutes on your face while trying to make it stick on your forehead and cheeks. If when removed, the handkerchief is moist, your skin is more likely to be oily to mixed. If it is not moist, the skin is likely to be normal to dry. Please keep in mind that this test is not 100% reliable as the elasticity of your skin will have changed every 10 years since your birth.

After your daily skin care regime, based on your skin type you can apply your foundation. (Some beauty specialists include the foundation application as part of the skin care regime, but here we have chosen not to do so). Please apply it onto your neck, ears, and eyelids too! Your foundation can be liquid, powder or compact. Apply it preferably with your fingers to all the surface of your skin including into the nostrils and under the eyes. For these a liquid camouflage concealer has to be considered with a medium coverage to start with. For dark skins, the "bronze" range is more likely to be closer to skin tones. Concealers aim at covering spots, wrinkles, birth scars, stretch marks, tattoos and, scars.

In general, concealers are close to foundations in texture and appearance. The only main difference is that concealers have higher pigment concentration with mineral oils to ensure a long lasting effect after their application. Available on the market in sticks, tubes and creams …it is recommended to buy them in two shades, for summer and a winter as we tend to go darker or lighter according to the season. Buying two concealers means buying two foundations too.Never use a concealer of the same colour or a darker shade than your foundation. This would draw attention to part of your face you wish to hide. In ancient Egypt white lead mixtures gave a bronze coloured foundation, used on special occasions. Made with fat from chickens, geese and bears, their cosmetics had the primary function of protecting the face from the desert sand. Differentiating men from women was secondary: only women were allowed to use several colours on their faces.

Mineral powder is not a modern invention. It has always existed in a in an old form used since ancient times. The ancient Egyptians expounded the benefits of using clay, talc and khôl on the human epidermis. Nowadays, consumers are much more aware of the relationships between skin problems and excessive daily absorption of chemical products from pollution and bad beauty products.

The benefits of using mineral powders are numerous: the skin is protected from the moment it is applied and it can be formulated for sensitive skin even in the case of cancer patients. It prevents blocked pores and acne. It has anti-inflammatory properties and as it is natural it is biodegradable.

Our final pieces of practical information about contemporary skin care are dedicated to body perfumes, eau de toilette and lotions. Using perfumed is the final touch to our daily beauty routine. Body odours tend to reveal our personalities by exposing our favourite scents. In the past, elegant and refined women used to keep one scent for a lifetime. Nowadays, there is a multiplicity of fragrances suitable for the modern lifestyle and a new aspect of beauty can be experienced through the nose. The range of fragrances differs according to the season, age, time, activity and ...femininity.

The main difference between perfume for men and for women is found in the tiny elements inside the perfume. Men's scents have a strong concentration of wood (musc) and lemon while women's scents are much more floral. Perfumes have been used, as part of skin care regime, since ancient Egyptian times. The first official historical evidence of perfume use can be dated back to 1000 BCE. Rose water, hibiscus oil or bissap was the first to be used. Made of a mixture of water, alcohol and perfumed oil, several types of perfumes are available. Water-based perfumes are the least co centrated and in time became the trade mark of the French industry. Fragranced waters aim at refreshing while delicately and discretely perfuming the body. Mature women and sportswomen are the keenest users. Included in this category are aftershave lotions as they are made of only 0,5% to 2% of perfumed oil. They have the advantage of being able to be sprayed all over the body at anytime during the day. They can last up to three hours under humid and hot conditions. Orange blossom is one of best examples of flower fragrances. Analysing active ingredients and their effects on human dermis may be illustrated by three examples within the beauty sector: hair, nail and perfume related cosmetics. We will briefly introduce the purpose of understanding cosmetology and chemistry to examine fully how people in ancient Egypt used to create their beauty products and how nowadays Western societies have adapted the original formulas.

Organic chemistry is the study of the composition, properties, preparation and structure of compounds made of molecules of carbons or hydrocarbons whether man-made or existing in nature.[38]Functional groups[39] are related to organic chemistry. Focusing on certain functional groups can help us identify from their chemical reaction, the effects these compounds may have on human skins. Alkanes for example ($C11\ H2n+2$) are in the functional group mainly found in paraffin wax and its effect on human skin is to moisture and repel. Alkenes ($R2C=CR2$) are found in creams and lotions and known for their anti-oxidant properties. Alcohols ($RO-H$) are often found in skin care creams and tend to dry out the skin or hair. Aldehydes are found in fragrances, as organic compounds and enhance natural odours occurring in vanillin and cinnam aldehydes. Esters are found in essential oils with similar properties as aromatic hydrocarbons and aromatics. The chemical reaction processes and its effects on dermis are the consequences of several factors. As explained in the previous chapter dedicated to the African hair type care, hair tends to react specifically to two groups of substances: acids and alkalis[40]. As pH, measures the activity of the hydrogen ion concentration on matter. In cosmetology, pH helps measuring the level of acidity of both products and skin, allowing professionals to evaluate the effects of chemical reaction on hair/skin therefore adjusting their treatments. pH is measurable on a scale from 0 to 14. Solutions with pH less than 7 are acidic and the ones above 7 being branded as alkaline. Functional groups with direct effects on pH level are numerous among chemical compounds. Strong acids such as phosphoric, sulphuric or hydrochloric acids are heavily used

---

38. http://en.wikipedia.org/wiki/Organic_chemistry

39. In organic chemistry, functional groups are specific groups atoms or bonds within molecules known to be responsible for the specific chemical reactions of those molecules

40. p stands for power and H for hydrogen - http://en.wikipedia.org/wiki/pH

in soap less detergents with a pH from 1 to 2; these compounds do burn human dermis[41].

Carboxylic acids (CH3COOH or CH3CO2H) are a functional group which acts as a PH adjuster in the making of esters. Similarly the amines (functional group found in shaving creams, face powders and hair colouring) also act as PH adjuster. Amides are organic compounds found in urea and responsible in cosmetology for colour uniformity and as stabilizers. Finally, the process of oxidation is one of the most popular chemical reactions created to develop cosmetics, defined as "a chemical process that involves combining a substance with oxygen ..."[42]; Oxygen molecules during a(quasi)-permanent colouring procedure enter the cortex, originating from hydrogen peroxide. Hydrogen gets into the cortex of the hair and destroys the melanin. Hydrogen is removed from the cortex by a neutralizer or conditioner which restores pH balance to its natural level (4.5-5.5). Active ingredients in beauty products also known as activators, are defined as "something that sets something else in motion or causes a reaction ..."[43]. Typically sculptured nails or acrylic nails are in fact liquid added to (acrylic)powder to form an activator (mould or nail). Another example of active ingredients in action would be the apigenin which is an activator used in chamomile vegetable dyes. Selenium sulphide and zinc pyrithione (also known as zinc omadine) is an active ingredient present in anti-dandruff shampoos while lawsone is another activator found in henna dyes[44]. Mainly present in hair products, active ingredients such as sodium, oralcium or potassiumhydroxides are commonly the compounds responsible for the relaxing process in African hair type perms. Because of the high risks of skin irritation experienced while using these chemicals, they tend to have been replaced in Lye relaxers by a formula mixing calcium hydroxide with guanidine carbonate to create guanidine hydroxide, softer to the human scalp[45].

41. *Hairdressing Science* by Florence Openshaw (Longman 1982)

42. *Illustrated Hairdressing Dictionary* p94 (Pearson 2008)

43. *Illustrated Beauty Therapy Dictionary* by Susan Cressy p3 (Heinemann 2008)

44. *Hairdressing science* by Florence Openshaw p. 253-256 (Longman 1982)

45. *Afro Hair Procedures and Techniques* by Ginger Browne p. 12 (Hyperion 1989)

Considering man-made and synthetic ingredients acting as aesthetic agents (created to enhance the product's sensory uniqueness), active ingredients such as titanium dioxide (mainly found in white powder sold by make-up companies) can also be replaced by a bleaching cream. Hydrogen peroxide hydroquinone is then used as a melanin reducing agent or activator of an oxidation process similar to the hair colouring procedure[46]. In the case of synthetic ingredients, the cosmetic industry has developed a wide range of esters[47] and esthers derived from natural perfumes found in plants, flowers and animals. While essential oils are not soluble in water but in alcohol, perfumes are therefore perfumed oils melted in alcohol and blended with water. Animal perfumes such as musk are extracted from a male musk deer while beavers and whales are excellent sources of perfumes found in nature. Man-made perfumes include phenyl ethyl alcohol (rose perfume) or benzyl acetate (floral perfume) and differ from organic esters by their irritating side effects such as olfactory fatigue, vomiting, hyperactivity, irritability, rashes or dizziness. Ancient Egyptians were known to stain "...their nails, the palms of their hands and the soles of their feet a reddish orange with henna, accented veins on the breast and temples with blue, and sometimes even painted their nipples ..."[48]. This leads us to clarify that skin care does include make-up application which starts with the foundation and stops once you have removed all traces of make-up on your face using a cleanser. The following natural beauty formulas may be used as guidelines to introduce the reader to the ingredients that provided delicateand simple understanding of skin care at its very early stages in the laboratory. Before undertaking any further action, check if you have any contra-indication or allergy.

e) Unavoidable Simple Safe Ingredients (USSI)

Herbs (green tea, ginseng).Clay (white, red, green and grey). Oils (olive, castor, coconut and argan). Exfoliators (sea salt, sugar

---

46. *Science for the Beauty Therapist* by John Rounce p.194 (Nelson Thornes 1983)

47. Chemical compounds made of a carbonyl molecule and an ether bond

48. *Manners and Customs of the the Ancient Egyptians* by Sir J.G.Wilkinson

and oats). Bicarbonate of soda; Aloe vera; organic honey; creamy yoghurt or *Petit Suisse* cheese; powdered milk; eggs; all dairy products; lemons; onion; garlic; cocoa powder; fruit, vegetables, spices, water. All these ingredients are the softer for the skin for those who do no longer wish to experiment any further.

2) HYGIENE & SAFETY

Always meet or talk to a qualified beauty professional (beautician, beauty therapist, aroma therapist, nail specialist, hairdresser, masseuse). Make sure she or he has an up to date insurance policy so as to reduce the risks of intense stress if an unwanted event occurs if you decide to carry out your own skin care in the home. Always test a small sample your new home made beauty product at home on your own skin for at least 24 hours before applying it elsewhere or offering it to anyone including friends and relatives. Only use glass or terracotta containers (the most natural available) to store your new beauty products. Always work in an airy kitchen with sufficient daylight and try to use spring water when preparing your formula to avoid any adverse or unexpected reactions. Never practice or apply your own beauty products on children, elderly people or pregnant women unless they have checked with their doctor! This is extremely important as their bodies are the most vulnerable to bacteria.

The following formulas serve as an introduction to ancient African beauty treatments which have been adapted to contemporary realities: milk powder or virgin oils replace the age old practices of soaking and extracting natural elements.

Some useful formulas

1) MASK FOR MATURE SKIN - Ingredients: a half avocado, 1 large spoonful of Greek style yogurt, 1 egg yolk.

People with mature and dry skins experience tightness on the face after washing. Their skin does not easily absorb liquid foundations which make them look as if they are wearing masks. It also tends to be hypersensitive around the eyelids or where the skin is thin or exposed to the elements and it peels or cracks.

2) SENSITIVE SKIN MASK -Ingredients: 1/2 banana, ¼ avocado, a large spoonful of honey (5ml), 1 large spoonful of argan oil.Sensitive skins are often allergic to mainstream, mass produced beauty products. They are very sensitive on the forehead and cheeks where the skin is more exposed to pollution and climate. It is time to return to natural remedies.

3) INTENSIVE MASK FOR DRY SKIN - Ingredients: 1/2 avocado, 5ml aloe vera juice

4) INTENSIVE MASK FOR NORMAL SKIN - Ingredients: 1 large spoonful of fruit juice (pineapple, mango or orange), 4 teaspoons of white clay, 2 teaspoons of mashed mango, 2 teaspoons of mashed banana, 2 teaspoons of milk powder, 1 teaspoon of honey

5) EXFOLIATORS - Ingredients: 4 spoonfuls of boiled oats, 2 spoonfuls of ginseng, 4 spoonfuls of olive, argan or coconut oil.

6) HAND AND FOOT CARE - In order to avoid dry feet, take a lemon, an onion or garlic, cut it into two pieces and apply it directly onto the dry or dead skin. Let it work on your skin. It is highly recommended to alternate between onion, lemon and garlic during the day as your skin's acidity changes throughout the day.

7) WEEKLY MASKS - Masks based on food are ideal for a weekly programme. Use egg, yogurt and various types of clay (white clay for dry to sensitive skins, green for oily skins and red for combination skins.).

8) IDEAS FOR LIPS AND CHEEKS - 45gr of raw beetroot, 3 large spoonfuls of vegetable glycerine.

PART III : BODY ADORNMENT AND MODIFICATION

1) MAPPING CULTURES

Body adornment is a cultural process aiming to dress and beautify the human body. Body adornment is generally taught as part of Western culture divided into two categories: dressing the body and modifying it. In this chapter we will analyse how for the ancient Africans dressing the body could also be performed by modifying it. Body adornment includes firstly the techniques of temporary visual body modification(also known as dressing) and secondly permanent body modification. These practices aim at results which allow the embellishment and identification of individuals through their appearance. Body adornment includes: clothing (dressing), hairdressing (temporary modification), make-up (temporary modification), tattooing (temporary or permanent modification), piercing (permanent modification), scarification (permanent modification), and dying or tinting (temporary modification). Note here that we use the word "make-up" to mean the application of anything other than water, fruit and vegetables onto the human dermis. We are not introducing here the insertion of objects into the dermis (also known as encumberment) which is really just a special piercing technique

Evolving in hot, humid climates, some human groups developed self-awareness and ways of dressing which would effectively protect their bodies from the excessive sun, dust, dirt, insects and body odours. Others, evolving in cold climates, developed focusing to protect their bodies from cold, humidity and also from society, sexuality and other people. These dressing needs are inherent in human beings whatever their social, cultural and historical development. Individuals have been able to express themselves by controlling their personal hygiene, first as part of a family and then within a social group, clan or gender. In time as the group widens and the individuals have experimented with different adornment techniques, the group ends up with a common beauty strategy.

Identification through the clothing, styling of hair and make up links the individual with his history and his social and economic condition.Thus a common visual and social identity came into existence. According to Michel Foucault, in organized state structures power was demonstrated through the appearance of the bodies of those supervising and disciplining society and through self-regulation. The most significant examples of such practices in ancient and pre-colonial Africa, are body modifications which explain themselves.

2) IDENTIFICATION OF DRESSING PRACTICES ON A GEOGRAPHICAL BASIS

Tattooing and scarification are both evidence of the experiences and challenges of life. The pain caused by these processes reflects the courage and strength of the person concerned and even his advancement in society. For skin which is bare or undecorated, Yoruba people, for example, prefer scarification as it marks the body forever as evidence of being part of a family. Berbers prefer facial tattoos which place the person within his socio-culture context for life. As Pierre Bourdieu explains in his 1980 book *Distinction: a Social Critique of the Judgment of Taste* hese practices are indicators not only of social class but of the entire social structure in relation to individuals' physical characteristics: height, shape or colour. Berbers in North Africa are renowned for their tattoo patterns and techniques which are a kind of archive passed down from mother to daughter only. Tattoos are considered to be talismans, and facial tattoos and face painting are curative and protective. These designs are mainly performed on the nose, under the mouth and around the eyes. Wearing silver jewellery follows the same ancestral tradition and, as well as being beautiful, is believed to provide protection and cure illness. These practices are more frequent at the time of important events in a woman's life such as puberty, marriage, pregnancy and childbirth. The *siyala* is a range of tattoo and scarification designs and patterns specifically targeting certain parts of the body to protect them spiritually from evil. Perceived as the most feminine design, the palm is heavily decorated with tattoos as it symbolically represents fertility and how many children a young woman could expect to have. The bare feet are also decorated as they need protection from evil spirits who might follow the young women's footprints. The eyes, mirrors of the soul, are the part of the body most at risk. They are surrounded with protective patterns to keep away evil spirits. *Siyala* thus has many functions: embellishment, destruction of evil forces and strengthening of good ones.

According to sociologist Margo DeMello in her *Encyclopedia of Body Adornment,* ancient Egyptians had similar decorative practices of tattooing, scarification and cosmetics for women. Tattooing seems to have been introduced by the Nubians in the pre-pharaonic era. The mummy of Amunet, a priestess of Hathor, had fertility patterns on her stomach and arms, mainly dots and dashes and an oval design. Scarification patterns were also found on female mummies. From the *siyala* and from ancient Egypt we can understand that tattooing practices were always significant for the entire group practicing them. As still practised - and only for women - tattooing and scarification in modern Africa can only be explained through spiritual and aesthetic culture.

Many other cultures across the African continent have managed to create their own codes of identification and beauty criteria. Ethiopia has several cultures which have adopted techniques of long term body modification. The nomads whose lifestyles are mainly based on cattle rearing and who have strong bonds between the members of the group are more likely to need to identify themselves with body markings. One of the most notable groups are the Mursi, a nomadic shepherd people who have scars on arms and bodies as a proof of personal achievement and social prestige. The chosen ones get married the same year. The Surma use scars when resolving conflicts. These fights are set up among different neighbouring groups in order to prevent potential future conflicts. If two men quarrel the community prepares them for a symbolic fight using sticks. The scars are to show to which group the fighter belongs. The Bumi have facial scars and colour their hair with different coloured clay.For the Karo people body painting is linked to the man's role at different stages in his life. Karo men go through three stages: childhood during which they watch the herds of cattle and perform minor tasks; later they have to protect the community; and finally as adults they can start a family, build up their own herds and educate the children. Each section of the population has body painting which is a kind of social identity card. Karo women have similar rules but they can only be fully scarred after marriage.

Bororo (Wodaabe) men who live in the Sahel region as well as in Nigeria and Cameroon during their famous annual festival, the *Geerewol*, men wear a kind of make-up to enhance their beauty in order to attract the eyes of women. Similarly Kaleri women in Nigeria have a real language with their scars. They are scarred after each important life event: birth, first menstruation, their first child and once they finish breastfeeding their scarification is complete. The famous Nuba people of South Sudan have an unlimited number of decorations for their bodies. The only rules relate to colours: initiated people are the ones allowed to use black. From the age of eight, girls can start applying red and white. Young men can also, once reaching puberty, wear yellow. Nuba men and women rub themselves with oil twice a day. This is their beauty secret.

3) MODIFYING THE BODY

a) Bodies and cultures.

Body art, the idea of beautifying the body by modifying it, has seen a spectacular popular revival since the 1970s when Western societies began to change attitudes of reserve, shame and disregard of the human body. This was illustrated by the punk and rasta movements as well as the development of art galleries and museums dedicated to dress. In 1975 the prestigious International Council of Museums (based at UNESCO) began to recognize organisations specialized in the history of fashion as members, including the Costume Society in the UK and the Costume Society of America. These changes are reflected in attitudes in today's globalized world. However, traditional Western ideals of beauty – youth, purity and cleanliness – were opposed (and still are) to permanent body modification practices. They tend to oppose permanent body modification. Changes to the skin or the body and scarification are associated with lack of proper care, disease, delinquency or perversion. How would you explain a gash or a scar if it is not the result of illness or of a violent attack? Exposure to such body modifications suggests the person is a social outcast or a criminal. According to sociologist Victoria Pitts in her book *In the Flesh,* she explains that body modification practices among youth and women are the most socially challenging and unacceptable as they tend to be automatically associated by the media with social deprivation and insecure environments. Sexual orientation is also associated with body modification: the skin is a link as well as a barrier between the inner and outer self. What a person desires and what he likes can be shown on his body. These perceptions about the relation between person and body reflecting moral and societal values deeply engrained in the Western culture.

Tattooing as a common practice is mentioned several times in the Bible in the Old Testament (Isaiah 44 verse 23). The text explains that ancient Hebrews used to tattoo their bodies as a symbol of their belief in one God or to mark burials and deaths. Tattooing is also mentioned in Leviticus 19 verse 28 in which God forbade Hebrews to practice it. The apostle Paul states in Galatians 6 verse 17 that he bears "the marks of Jesus" to remember the pain endured by Christ. Regarding the habit of piercing the ears and nose, Leviticus 19 verse 28 reads: "Do not cut your bodies for the dead or put tattoo marks on yourselves." They were certainly wearing gold earrings as shown when Moses' brother Aaron collects them to make the golden calf (Exodus 32). Deuteronomy 15 verse 17 and Exodus 21 verse 6 show that nose and ear rings were given to slaves or servants to indicate their status. Finally Genesis 24 verse 22 confirms that nose piercing existed before the time of the ancient Hebrews.

In some parts of Africa, elongating the neck, stretching earlobes or inserting plates in the lips and genitals are examples of practices to modify and reshape the body. The Mursi and Surma in Ethiopia, the Sara in Chad, the Lobi in Ghana and the Kirdi in Cameroon are some of the peoples who practice the insertion of plates in the lips. They do this to show bravery and because for them it is beautiful. Unmodified skin is to them like an empty canvas. A person who is not tattooed or scarred is unattractive and his or her culture is not visible. Such a person is not courageous enough to bear the pain endured during the insertion of objects into the skin or by tattooing or scarring.Only outcasts and criminals would keep themselves unidentified.

In Europe, at the time of the Roman Empire, the order of Centurions, a group of elite military officers, used to pierce their nipples to identify themselves in relation to other military groups. They could also tie their heavy capes in place using their pierced nipples! Archeologists have found evidence of tattooing tools which shows that tattooing in Europe dates back 40,000 years, long before the time of the Romans. Ancient talismans have been found which prevented pain, probably associated with these practices. In the Middle Ages, after the Crusades the Inquisition forbade tattooing, labeling it; archaic and satanic. Today many in Western societies oppose it.

b) Modifying the body for social reasons

Tattooing in the past has always been confined to prisoners, sailors, soldiers and the working classes. Jean-Chris Miller in his book *The Body Art* explains that the upper classes would go for a more elaborate and artistic designs. The ancient Greeks, Romans and Persians used to mark the bodies of their runaway slaves showing the type of punishment they had experienced or the crime committed. Thus marked on the most visible parts of their body, their faces and hands, the offenders could be identified wherever they went. Similarly, during the 2,000 years of black slavery Arab and Europeans slave traders adopted the same type of practices on their slaves. (Slavery only; became illegal in Yemen in 1967). Arab slave owners specialized in castration and torture; blacks, as soon as they had been captured, shaved and converted to Islam, were castrated to prevent them from reproducing, a practice equivalent to genocide: most eunuchs in the region were and still are black Africans. Women were systematically raped and forced to marry the rapists. The children born from these forced unions were automatically converted to Islam. The principal victims of the trans-Sahara slave trade were the African women who were kidnapped, brutalized and marked for life, having their very humanity denied as they faced slavery, rape and daily violence.

In the same period, prisoners began copying criminals and designing tattoos onto their skins and tattooing became more widespread. Sometimes, prisoners and criminals would try to change the original design to conceal its problematic origin. Later, prisoners would create their own designs showing their affiliation to a group, their social position or their crime. Today despite the fact that tattooing is prohibited in US prisons, it happens nonetheless and not always voluntarily (see *Encyclopedia of Body Adornment* by Margo DeMello). Branding was also a common practice in ancient Greco-Roman times.The Greek letter, delta, or letter "D" was branded on slaves, referring to the word *doulos* (slave). The letter "F" meant fugitive. Similar practices were used by trans-Atlantic and trans-Sahara slave traders. Similarly the Canadian army branded deserters with a "D" or "BC" for bad character. The British army branded "D" on deserters' foreheads "T" for thief. "TF" was commonly used in France for *travaux forcés* (forced labour).

We have seen that slavery, imprisonment, branding, castration, torture, and tattooing are body changing punitive practices.

c) Body modification as spiritual protection

To this list we could add female genital mutilation and breast ironing. These practices have been used in patriarchal societies in some countries to control women's sexuality by forcing them to deny it. A sexually active woman, if she had unlimited sexual pleasure, would be tempted to be unfaithful to her husband and bear someone else's children. Therefore, the "best" prevention was to remove the "satanic" part of her body which would eventually lead her to sin. In Cameroon, breast ironing is used to slow down the growth of the breasts has long been practiced among women in remote parts of the country where life is a permanent economic challenge. This would make the girl look too young to attract the eyes of men. This would protect her girl from getting pregnant at an early age and destroy all her chances of a better life. The physical and psychological effects of such practices are irreversible. Often conducted by women who have been raised to accept the patriarchal African society in which they have evolved, these "preventive" practices through punishment are an absolute denial of women's sexuality. Statistically the phenomenon represents 26% of Cameroonian girls. Cameroon, being a country of Bantu majority including the Tikkar (who have populated the South West region of Cameroon over the last thousand years), women and men were traditionally and initially equal in rights and sexuality. A good example is recorded by German explorer Gunther Tessman in 1921.[49] The Bafia people of the Central region of Cameroon (Mbam) are among some of the few people of Tikar origin and Bantu lineage. Until the earliest part of the 20th century, their lifestyles were still relatively close to their original Bantu traditions. During the period of German rule Presbyterian missions tried to segregate people who were still worshiping their original God and the Bafia used to raise their children with a mixture of their traditions and the Western beliefs. As a result, Bafia people were Christianized rather than really converted. Christianization included having biblical first names. Their initial tradition was to adopt the father's name next to the child's own name (which itself was often a forefather's name chosen to reinforce the child's belonging to a clan or family bloodline). Christianization also included getting baptized and speaking either Bulu, a coastal language which was used by Germans and Portuguese settlers, or - for the most gifted children - German. This process of both Westernization and Christianization led to an entire generation of young people willing to add these "new" ways of life onto their original lifestyle. This allowed the lowest classes which were always favoured by the colonialists to advance socially within the colonial environment. Being the only ones educated to read both Bulu and German and to understand the religion of the colonial power, they became the "elite" in charge of the local administration. They and the colonialists both wanted to defeat the ruling families which were still had moral authority and which were allowing freedom for men and women to choose their partners (often based on both physical features or characteristics and bloodlines). They banned women from puberty

49. *Boy-Wives and Female Husbands: Studies in African Homosexualities,* ed. Stephen Murray & Will Roscoe. (St. Martin's Press 1998)

to choose potential life partners at the same time as making school compulsory for girls up to the age of 14. The official reason for this was to "educate" women about chastity while disciplining men regarding their libido. Traditionally sexuality was widely explained to children as early as 5 years old and sexual games among young people were tolerated until puberty; women were separated from men as soon as their bodies were transforming mainly to avoid unwanted and early pregnancies. After the French and British took control of Cameroon after the German defeat in the First World War, the population was partly converted, partly Christianized and very few were "full" ancestor worshippers. Stopping the girls getting married young was a way of protecting them from getting pregnant to avoid poverty or dying young due to lack of medical treatment and limited access to hospitals. In this context the practice of breast ironing was introduced from the 1940's.

Similarly, according to a recent interview given by Waris Dirie[50] to an African lifestyle magazine, 28 African countries are still legally accepting the Female Genital Mutilation (FGM) as an established practice. Somalia, Burkina Faso, Uganda and Togo are among the few African countries who have forbidden FGM of all types. 140 million women in the world have been victims of these practices and 3 million young girls every year in Africa are subject to FGM. To fully understand the phenomenon, we will try to establish the "origins" of this habit. Sexual rites are perceived in many contemporary African societies as beautification, as rites of passage and sometimes as rites of intensification. As a form of body modification or surgery, female genital circumcision includes four types of transformation[51]: partial or total excision of the *labia minora*, the excision of the prepuce or part of the clitoris, and finally the infibulation (excision of part or all of the external genitalia including narrowing and sometimes stitching of the vaginal opening) and finally FGC which stands for female genital cutting

---

50. Arise Magazine issue 18 (January 2013)

51. www.forwarduk.org.uk: The Foundation for Women's Health, Research and Development. FORWARD- is an African Diaspora women's campaign and support charity (registered in the UK) founded in 1983

and piercing practices. The most popular among these practices is the infibulation also known as the "Pharaonic circumcision"[52].

From a religious point of view, Muslims are divided according to the schools or orthodox rites in Islam they follow. The *makruma*[53] is not compulsory for women. Marie Assad (1982) suggested that Shafites, Malikites, Hanafites and Hanbalites have different views and opinions on how to understand and apply *fatwas*[54]. Hanafites and Hanbalites see the Makruma as a *sunna*[55]. Malikites consider it as an embellishment for women and an obligation for men while the Shafites view the practice as compulsory for both men and women. For Sudanese women practitioners[56], the FGM is a mapping of gender (feminity), sexuality (it limits lesbianism), geography (ethnically mapping the women) and finally spiritual (purifying the body). These principles of branding women in their flesh are forms of body communication sent to the world surrounding these men and women: assuggested by Mark Tungate in his concept of branding pyramid (see below)[57]

Logo

Logo
|
Look & Feel
|
Targeted messages
|
Core messages
|
We know who we are

---

52. According to Linguist Abdella Eltayes after having analysed the 1991 demographic health survey estimations

53. Circumcision of young girls

54. An Islamic religious and legal pronouncement often issued by a religious authority

55. Similar to a religious recommendation

56. The 1991 demographic health survey estimations

57. *Fashion Brands: Branding Style from Armani to Zara* by Mark Tungate (Kogan ,2005)

Neither traditional nor cultural, FGM and FGC are methods of body adornment to enhance a woman's sense of womanhood according to those who perform it.

It is interesting to notice that according to Ben Barker-Benfield[58], during the late 19th century and early 20th century clitorectomy was a medical solution to fight excessive libido and masturbation among women, while castration and circumcision were allowed as remedies to fight hysteria, insanity and epilepsy. American, French, German and British women used to be genitally mutilated during the 19th century as a way of preventing them being sexually insatiable! The advent of psycho-analysis would eventually stop the painful "cure".

58. *The horror of the half-known life* by Michael Kimmel (Routledge,2000)

IMAGES GROUP I: HAIR

Queen Tiye of 18th Dynasty - Egypt

A Hinba woman in
Nambia,photo Runoko

I

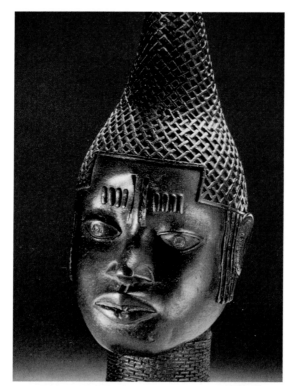

Ethiopian Hair Style
vs Ancient Egyptian
hair Style

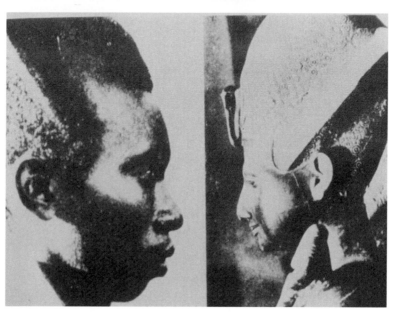

Head of man - ancient Benin

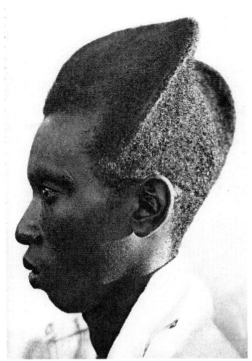

Himba men hair style

Kongo man 1935 by K.
Zagourski

Kongo man 1935 by
K. Zagourski

Kongo man 1935 by
K. Zagourski

Original Ethiopian hairdressing

V

Somali man

Tutsi hairdressing 1935

Hair style - Cameroon

Hair style - Cameroon

IMAGES GROUP II: SKIN - BODY PAINTING

Body painting, Mangbetu Queen - Agostino Arts

Kongo woman 1935 by K. Zagourski

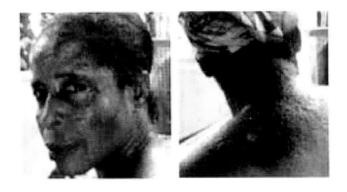

Skin bleach

IMAGES GROUP III: SCARIFICATION

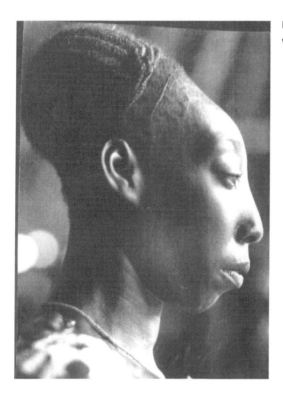

Head of Mambegtu
Woman DRC

Head of Tutankhamun, eldest example of Lopombo

Head of Woman in ancient Kingdom of Benin (modern Nigeria)

Nuer man and Woman in south Sudan, photo Runoko

Head of Ife king

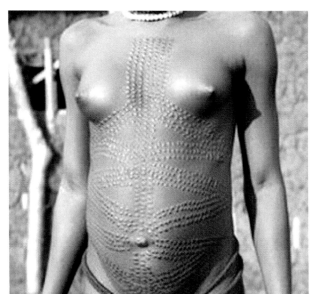

Cameroon girl
- Circa 1930

Old woman in Congo
1930

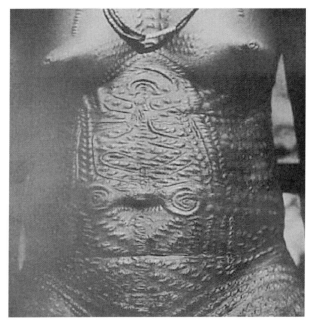

Scarification

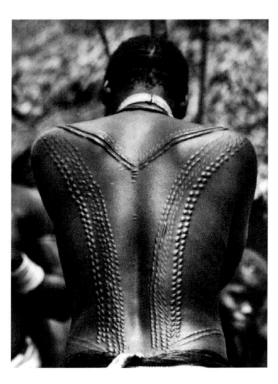

Bwaka Woman
Circa 1930

Scarification 1918

A Dinka man in South Sudan - photo Runoko

IMAGES GROUP IV: BODY ADORNMENT - TEXTILE

Baboko 1916

Bamenda Clothes Cameroon

A Bulu man 1916

A noble Bana 1916

An East African soldier

A family photo - roots

A Fulbe man 1916

Tutsis sports party 1935

Wrapping of mummies in
Ancient Egypt

African Nudes Meetup RAW
photo C. Kedi

The Amazons vetreans form Abomey - Dahomey

Maasai Men, Kenya

Bamenda clothes Cameroon

Angela - photo C. Ked

Creoles head wrapping

Young Fulbe girl 1917

Young Hausa girl 1917

IMAGES GROUP V: ACCESSSORIES

Ancient Rwanda man

A Baboute 1916

Warriors in Ancient Benin Kingdom

A Bamun Woman 1916

Bana man, 1916

Berber woman from
Morocco

A Dinka Woman in South Sudan, photo Runoko.jpg

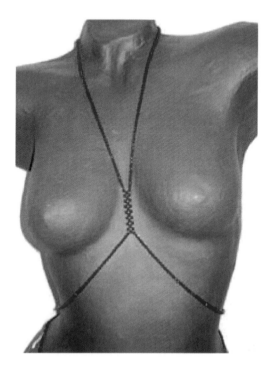

Jal Jali photo C. Kedi

Head of soldier
Ancient Benin Photo
C, Kedi

Tutankhamun (1336 BC - 1327
BC

Fatou-fatal-Collection- C.Kedi

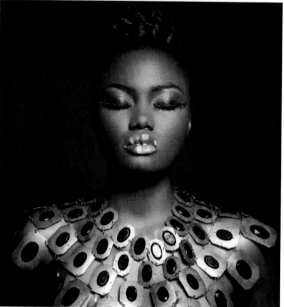

"Nefertiti" Photo C. Kedi

PART IV: TEXTILES: BODY ADORNMENT THROUGH COLOURS.

1) COLOUR

Colour is an integral part of an electromagnetic spectrum. Rays of colour originate in darkness or from somewhere imperceptible to the human eye. This identification by colour happens at a very early stage in human life: newborn babies acquire this ability before they can even see different shapes. Very few mammals and other creatures have the ability to see the entire colour spectrum as humans can. Some species such as cats can see certain colours which humans cannot see. Tortoises can see the same range of colours as humans and their longevity has created in Bantu culture either a fear or an ultimate respect for tortoises. It is also well known that children at a young age like to choose a favourite colour. This sensitivity to colour has led to research on alternative therapies based on how colour affects an individual's personality:

the tints and tones may express one or more states of the aura or *karma* or the level of mental vibration experienced at the time of the analysis. Our individual or collective reaction to colour will influence our behaviour in society. Colours have had influence on cultures and civilizations throughout history.

Our reaction to colours can also reveal our innate nature or esoteric reality. The universal code of colours, used by colour theorists and therapists, can heal individuals according to the visual energy attributed to each colour. Messages sent through daylight are automatically received by human eye as colours or shadows. The interaction of daylight and colour sends two types of signal to the visual cortex in the brain which will then interpret these signals according to its needs. This process will create another interaction with the entire human brain which will operate two types of stimulation, of colour and of light. At this stage, colour can give humans two things: a conscious method of communication related to cultural and emotional symbols; and an unconscious method of communication which is related to light. These interpretations will add to those already existing inside the brain since infancy. It is at this very precise time that colour becomes associated with beliefs and concepts based on the cultural environment.

2) CIVILIZATIONS, COLOURS AND CULTURES

The Vedas are a collection of religious texts and chants revealed to wise men in ancient India. Also known as shruti (which means what is heard), they were written in Sanskrit around 1,500 BCE though previously they had been transmitted through oral tradition as the early Aryans did not possess a written language. The *Dharma sutra* and the *Dharma Shastras* are law books organizing the Hindu caste system and life in general. One of the best known *Shastras* is called the *Law of Manu*. The main character is the Hindu equivalent of Noah. These texts appeared between 500 BCE and 500 CE at the same time as Buddhism (which was still considered as a new religion at the time!). The Puranas are the epic and mythological texts relating the lives of the gods. Many other religious texts were added later. Those relating to "Abrahamic" characters such as Jesus Christ and Abraham are the ones we will consider closely. According to the *Bhagavad Gita* ("The song divine"), a central text for the Hindu religion with its 700 verses, Krishna – a figure as important as Jesus in a Western religious context or as Horus in ancient Egypt - is often represented with very dark blue or black skin, and he wears yellow silk. Hinduism originated in the Indus valley (in modern Pakistan) around 3500 BCE. Aryan invasions around 1500 BCE from the Hindu Kush are mainly responsible for the racially stratified caste system which still exists in India today. The *Vedas* were written under these two influences: Hinduism and the Aryans.

Aryans are described as tall, light skinned in the book, *"Arya"* written by Virender Kumar (2003). Understanding who the Aryans were historically will help us to understand the code of colours in modern India which is the only country in Asia where dark skinned people have been segregated because of the shade of their skin, as we will explain in the next chapter. Originally from central Asia, the Aryans started their movement to south Asia in two waves around 200 BCE. One group settled north of Greece and another in Iran (from which "Aryan" is derived). From these two initial destinations, a small group of Aryans decided to travel to India. Initially nomads and hunters, Aryans mastered the art of metallurgy and the making of weapons. Once the Aryans acquired some lands in India, they started animal rearing and agriculture. They spoke a primitive form of Sanskrit, were living in tribes subdivided into family clans. This how with time they started classifying the professions and creating a caste system. They started intermarrying with Hindus and adopted some of their purification rituals and hygienic practices before performing any religious acts. By 1000 BCE, the Aryan culture was already dominant in north India and their presence was recorded in the Ganges plain. The Brahmins, the literary elite in charge of the transmission of knowledge and of Hindu practices, felt threatened by the invasion of the "white" Huns and therefore accelerated the recording in Sanskrit language of the Vedas. They also took the opportunity to set up strict structures and social hierarchies to accommodate the fast growing population as well the arrival of new communities: sub-classes were born. The Vedic cult declined as Brahminic Hinduism grew involving ritual sacrifices to the gods.

The ancient Greek mythology leads us back to historic figures writers who wrote the epics of the Olympian gods among whom was Zeus, the supreme god living in the sky. According to the pre-dynastic Egyptian mythology, Nut, goddess of the sky and Geb god of the land conceived Isis and Osiris who were brother and sister. They married each other, for tradition dictated that gods, as they had perfect genes, had to marry among themselves. After he was defeated by Seth, the god of bad luck and chaos, during a fight, Osiris was cut into fourteen pieces and Isis, his wife, despite her inconsolable sorrow, decided to conceive a child from the remains of her husband's body and also to resuscitate Osiris himself. Horus, the child born of this miraculous conception was half human and half divine.

The colours most used in the pre-dynastic Egyptian mythology are archived in the sacred *Book of the Dead* as well as in the *Papyrus of Nu* (illustration number 10477, sheet 5) which refers to "red" for the first time as a red bird is seen on the deceased person's rite of passage to the after-life during which he has to face with three crocodiles. Red is again mentioned on (illustration no. 10477, sheet 8) when referring to Neti, "the god with the double red crown". Illustration 10477, sheet 11 mentions again a beer made of red seeds. This sheet shows the rules on food for the life after death. The most significant reference to the use of colour is on sheet 6 of the same illustration which refers to "red beings" who the only ones are allowed to see Osiris, a sacred being. The colour green is only mentioned in sheet 26 in the chapter on the four flames of the spirit. Green is only used in ceremonies. Green has to be mentioned because of the existence of green clay and it is only mentioned once. Turquoise appears twice and is associated with water in both these references. Red is sacred and a primary colour. Green is a mixture of yellow and blue and is a secondary colour.

3) UNDERSTANDING THE RAINBOW

a) The Colour Spectrum

We compare colours to food: if you prefer a certain type of food a nutritionist would usually say that you naturally tend to be attracted to it. A vegetarian would prefer eating anything but animal flesh. It is both a choice and a preference at the same time. The colour range for animal flesh is from dark pink through red to purple. Poultry would suggest a creamy colour. Plants with the same colours but with different textures which can affect the perception of colours for vegetarians.

Human reactions to the cultural use of colour are various: the Western tradition based on ancient Greek culture venerated creamy, white and neutral colours, as is witnessed by the enormous artistic heritage of Greece.

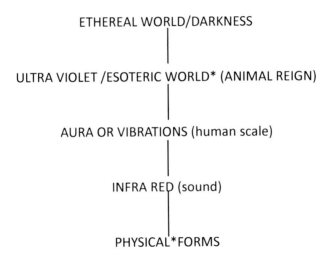

* From ethereal to sound perception

ETHEREAL WORLD/DARKNESS

ULTRA VIOLET /ESOTERIC WORLD* (ANIMAL REIGN)

AURA OR VIBRATIONS (human scale)

INFRA RED (sound)

PHYSICAL*FORMS

The word "ethereal" originates from "ether" which is defined as an essential organic component of the atom. It is an infinitely small molecule but containing complex codification which causes it to obey the rules of physics. Ether is smaller than an atom and is sub-divided into even smaller elements. Physical forms are the last stage of visual identification. Every single object seen by the human eye is made of atoms, substance and shades of colour. Understanding of the ethereal is important: it is central to the representation of the system of colours that the culture will try to codify. For the Sufis, ether is non-measurable and permanent. It is part of the creation process in order to perceive the reality of phenomena. On the contrary, what is physical or concrete is what is measurable and quantifiable.

In ancient Greek cultures, artistic representation could perceive a type of reality in all its splendour since their conception of beauty was based on the culture of the ephemeral and on the cult of eternal youth as a promise of beauty. The gods of Olympus such as Zeus were bearded but were depicted as muscular, without wrinkles and with bodylines close to an ideal of perfection. Even the stone and clay used to carve statues were selected to be durable: stone, clay - eternal gods do not degenerate or grow old; they have no colour- they are carved out of materials that are as pure as they are natural.

For the Nubians of the pre-dynastic era in ancient Egypt, beauty reflects not a physical reality but another esoteric and ethereal one as nothing exists without a soul, spirit or breath of life. This energy of movement and this creative energy are represented in their invisible purity which is, however, visible to artists who have been initiated into "orders" since colours were given to the gods. All the artists or artisans were members of orders which were co-operative schools and associations, similar to mediaeval guilds or religious orders of monks or nuns. These orders taught them to visualize and sometimes connect with degrees of imaginative energy which might appear as phantoms, visions of the past or the future or mysteries of one kind or another. For people in ancient Egypt, colour was used to treat physical or spiritual pain. The sufferer would go to temples specialized in using colour therapies. Having arrived at the temple he or she would choose four colours and the therapist would diagnose the light energies and base the treatment on the patient's state of mind and emotions. Four levels of colours enable the problem to be identified: the first would deal with physical problems (the body), the second with emotional ones (the heart), the third the mental problems (the brain) and finally the fourth colour would deal with spiritual problems (the soul). After the problems have been analysed, different techniques were either proposed or carried out on the patient, including "visualization". This is a natural human process which uses stimulation to recreate a colour in the mind. The emotions and stimuli resulting from this would cause physical reactions similar to the reactions inside the patient's body if he could see the colour in front of him. Thinking about one colour is the same as visualizing it.

This brings us back to the realization of the value that each person attributes to colour based on their personal experience.

The second method much used by the ancient peoples is called the projection of colour. It consists of projecting several colours to create a specific atmosphere in which the patient would be mentally and physically stimulated and eventually completely cured. Places like cathedrals, theatres and night clubs use this kind of technique and it can quickly affect people's feelings and put them in a good humour. The famous physicist Isaac Newton, translated the musical notes into the colours of the rainbow: indigo (A), violet (B), red (C), orange (D), yellow (E), green (F) and blue (G). Again, according to ancient mythology, yellow was a colour given to men by the gods and associated with the goddess Isis. (source: Encyclopedia of Mythology, 1919). Yellow stones and crystals were often used by ancient Egyptian people who believed that these crystals were the perfect example of the balance of physical matter in the universe, representing the three dimensions of colour, form and ethereal alignment.

Other more complex methods were also widely used. Modern colour therapists are still using some of these teachings to identify and diagnose discomfort among sufferers and to study the colour spectrum. Thus today many pathological conditions are being treated in this way as a form of alternative medicine.

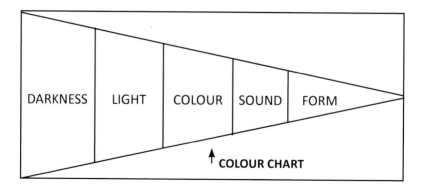

| DARKNESS | LIGHT | COLOUR | SOUND | FORM |

↑ **COLOUR CHART**

Getting familiar with the colour chart or colour wheel will enable you to understand how colours work and this will help you create harmony when your make-up or your clothes. The colours most used in the mythology of ancient pre-dynastic Egypt can be found in the *Book of the Dead* and the *Papyrus of Nu* (as seen in previous chapter).

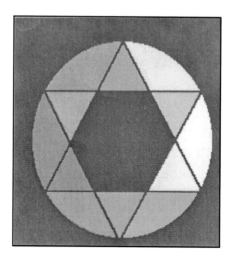

b) Primary colours

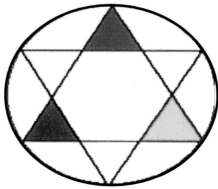

Our ability to react to colours results from an association of ideas, concepts and emotions with the light which contains colour. The different vibrations, radiations or frequencies of the light result in profound changes within the body regardless of the culture we belong to. Colour symbolism has its own language. In this way the language of colour has given birth to specialisms such as photography and the science and theory of colour. Primary colours, blue, red and yellow, are those that exist in nature and are fundamental to light processes. In this context we can analyse the symbolic significance of colours in different historical periods, cultures and social systems. The various colours form a kind of alphabet where each shade represents a different emotion.

Yellow is the primary colour associated with the immune, nervous and digestive systems and is the colour to relieve stress. It is a colour that focuses exclusively on the emotions and is associated with the solar plexus. This is why for example intense stress affects the stomach and up to the throat. In the Western world yellow is sometimes used to attract and keep customers by associating it to fast food and services in general. In ancient Kemet, yellow was already recognised as a primary colour and was used for painting. A normal yellow was obtained from ochre, which is derived from iron oxide. A pale yellow was obtained by mixing sulphur with beeswax.

Yellow was needed to create the colour gold which has relaxing and calming qualities and was used for beauty creams for skin care based on coloured flowers. It has a relaxing effect on the skin where it could have a repairing effect. In ancient Kemet it was much used in the process of making mummies. Also, due to its rarity and the interest it provokes, it gives confidence to the person wearing it. It is the colour of success.

Red is the primary colour with the lowest density and the least possible variation of shade. It creates a spiritual balance as it is the colour of blood and thus the symbol of life. Representing physical strength, it is used a lot in everyday life, for example in advertising food or cars or for sports teams. Red is also one of the three primary colours expressed by Osiris, the deity of the afternoon. For colour therapists, red is the colour used to manage tensions within the body. Obtained from iron oxide or ochre it was much used for wall

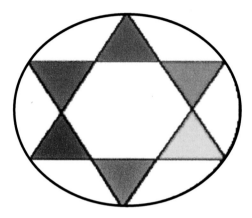

paintings and on bodies. Infra-red is half way between eyesight and hearing and is still sacred to many cultures today. It is, for example, the symbol of femininity in Chinese culture.

FATHER/<u>AMUM</u>/RED/<u>OSIRIS</u>

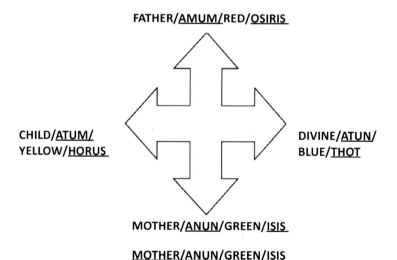

CHILD/<u>ATUM/</u>
YELLOW/<u>HORUS</u>

DIVINE/<u>ATUN/</u>
BLUE/<u>THOT</u>

MOTHER/<u>ANUN</u>/GREEN/<u>ISIS</u>

MOTHER/<u>ANUN</u>/GREEN/<u>ISIS</u>

Blue is the colour for intellectual activity. Unlike red it reduces blood pressure and has a relaxing effect. Its best association in nature is the sky which - even though air has no colour - we perceive to be blue, and this makes us feel relaxed. In ancient Egypt, blue was the colour of the god Thoth. Blue is the last colour before the sun sets and complete darkness (*atun*) descends. Only the light of the moon remains, awaiting the resurrection of the sun (*atum*) the next morning.

c) Secondary colours

When mixing different primary colours we create secondary colours: green (blue and yellow), orange (yellow and red) and purple (blue and red).

Green is one of the colours used in science as the fourth "psychological" colour. It is a symbol of perfect balance, the colour of nature which is easy on the eye in every context and culture. For ancient Egypt, green was the colour for *anun*, the female principle and it was the colour for maternity. Secret, feminine and hidden, green was also associated with Isis, the mother of Horus and the wife and sister of Osiris.

Orange is an equal mixture of red and yellow. It is the colour for creativity and liberation. Orange is associated with the lower part of the stomach and especially the large intestines and the reproductive organs. It is a colour often found in food and it helps to clear and relax the mind after shock, stress or trauma.

Purple is a mixture of blue and red (complementary colours) which gives it the attributes of both these colours: spiritual wellbeing – the sacred aspect coming from red and the intellectual from blue, linking with emotions such as sympathy and compassion. Purple is associated with the head and is supposed to be able to stimulate the two halves of the brain and create a balance between them.

Tertiary colours are a mixture of primary colours with secondary colours, turquoise for example which a mixture of blue and green is. Finally there are complementary colours are shown opposite each other on the colour wheel: red and green; blue and orange; yellow and purple.

Terminology[59].

"hue" enables an observer to classify a colour.

"tint" has a hint of white.

"shade" has a hint of black or indicates the darkness or lightness of the colour

"tone" is a tint with a hint of grey.

"chrome" is the presence of colour.

"saturation" (or "chromatic intensity") is the percentage of colour present.

"monochrome" combines shades, tones and nuances into one single colour.

"achromatism" means absence of colour such as white, black and grey.

d) Neutral shades

Black, white and grey are not really colours but "shades". Black contains all the colours of the spectrum apart from white and white contains all the colours apart from black. Grey is a mixture of both black and white. Black has no light and white has no darkness.

In Western tradition, black represents the spiritual depth of our souls, the hidden, the sacred, an uncertain and unknown venture into night or darkness. In the north, the sun's rays are shorter than in the tropics. In the moderate climate of western Europe the frequently cloudy sky makes night totally black and the stars invisible. Total night can mean illicit activities, criminality, insecurity and this is linked to our own emotions and experiences.

Blackness in many ways intimidates people in Western societies as it symbolizes the difficulty to explore the depths and secrets hidden in the dark. Black came to represent fear of the unknown and thus of darkness and negativity in general. The word for "black" in ancient Greek was *necro* which ended up in Latin as *niger*... νεκρός(*necros)* means "death or dead body" hence the English word "necrology". The derivatives of the word *niger* have given all forms that are used in the modern spoken languages derived from Latin as well as "negro" (and the pejorative "nigger") in English.

59. *How not to Wear Black* by Jules Standish

While European socio-cultural traditions were being established during the Middle Ages, a differentiation between traditional nobility and new nobility was reinforced by the code of dressing: psycho-symbolic values were added. White and black were worn by people of the highest rank and church people such as priests, monks or nuns. These two classes of nobles had a similar lifestyle with activities such as sewing and the many domestic tasks for the women and entertaining guests. They feared exposure to the sun, which darkened the skin of the serfs working in the fields. Staying "white" was a confirmation of their social rank. By contrast, court ladies in southern Europe exposed their heads so that the sun would bleach the roots of their hair, and they also used chamomile mixed with lime to aid the process. Blond hair became regarded as a sign of beauty.

Peasants and serfs were tied to the land where they worked. Serfs were "owned" by the knight or lord possessing the land. These "dark faces" reflected the social absolutism and determinism typical of feudalism and of the values of European (and Indian) societies in the Middle Ages. As with the transatlantic slave trade a few centuries later, social inferiority was based on dark skin and manual work outdoors while light skin appeared socially superior and represented freedom from physical hardship. In the Middle Ages and later churchmen were not expected to do manual work but there were huge social differences among the clergy: the village priest and the bishop had totally different lifestyles: but both had to wear black as a sign of their spiritual role, although red had symbolism for Christians too and is worn by Roman Catholic Cardinals. Another Western tradition is that black is a sign of mourning, especially for widows: Queen Victoria wore black for nearly forty years from the day her husband, Prince Albert, passed away until her own death. Upper class women would show off fine quality cloth such as silks and cottons imported from India or China. This trend of widows wearing black declined after the Second World War when the famous designer, Coco Chanel, created the little black dress wearable for anyone at any time of the day. For the Chinese, black is associated with water, perceived as something precious, both passive and constant.

White has no colour or shadow but it can also be controversial. After long being associated with purity, perfection and innocence and still present to this day in Judeo-Christian religious cultures, this association of ideas has justified the growth of racial and racialist ideologies. Before the end of the 19th Century Western bride did not wear white dresses but red or flowery dresses to symbolize joy. White became the established "colour" for brides to fit in with Victorian values at the time and to represent purity and virginity. Nowadays, white has a larger significance: cold, sterility, arrogance, isolation, emptiness and absence of compassion are among its negative sides. Both black and white contain an equal proportion of the three primary colours (yellow, blue and red). White symbolizes threats: the cold, the end of everything or death. At the same time, white helps to differentiate objects, things and beings. It is associated with cleanliness and can mark you out as different and separate from the crowd. White also represents total change or transformation. Black and white are the basis on which colours can be drawn or woven.

Brown is the colour of the soil and indicates stability and solidity. The earth is the source of life and the ground under our feet which makes it is also an excellent basis on which to add other colours. Being itself a mixture of red, yellow and blue, brown represents patience and practicality. People who think logically feel at ease with brown, as it is the colour for long term success.

4) COLOURS AND ADORNMENT

As their art shows, the people of ancient Egypt always tried to represent a person in the most favourable way with a healthy body, not too thin or too obese, no wrinkles or scars, white hair or varicose veins. It transcended the concept of true reality. The work of the ancient Egyptian sculptor, painter or embalmer was to magnify and even make mysterious the appearance of the deceased or beloved person. The body obeyed the rules in the *Papyrus of Ani*.

Udju: Used from the time of the earliest dynasties, *udju* was made from green malachite. It was considered as a gift from the Hathor, goddess of spirituality based on beauty, joy, love and women.

Mesdemet: This was a dark grey mineral derived from sulphide or from galenite. Widespread in Egypt, galenite was introduced into cosmetic practice by Queen Hatshepsut at the time of her celebrated expedition to the land of Punt.

Saffron: Used to colour the eyelids yellow. Saffron was highly regarded as it was rare and expensive.

Jasper: a mineral which was looted and used as a medicinal treatment for eye infections.

Burnt almond: used with different mixtures of mineral elements as it solidified them so they could be used for eye make-up.

a) Understanding textile language

Textiles identify the individual in his social context, integrating him into his culture by his socio-economic status and his prestige when at spiritual or religious gatherings. "Clothes are an ingredient of style, and serve to provide protection, to preserve our modesty, to convey our status and to create an impression"[60]. Marriages, initiation ceremonies and funerals are the most significant moments in the life of people living in Africa today. They are ceremonies at which the use of different textiles is most clearly codified and where African aesthetics have more influence over quality than form of dress. Textile art also plays a part in purely domestic and utilitarian products such as tents, hammocks and bedclothes. The way in which cloth is processed on the continent is the chief distinguishing feature which indicates the socio-geographical origin of a textile: raffia, silk, cotton or wool are variously used according to the climatic, environmental, economic and cultural contexts. Thus sheep's wool is very commonly worn in rural parts of the Maghreb and West Africa. Silk is chosen by the Malagasy, Ethiopians, Senegalese and people of the Maghreb. The modern textile industry has brought in more modern materials and

60. *How to win clients and interpret their needs* by Ian Mistlin (Blackwell Scientific 1994)

techniques but still respects ancestral traditions and customs. For example, in the Congo among the Bakuba-Shoowa people raffia is embroidered and worn to show off the wealth of a deceased person at the funeral, in areas where such material is seen as a sign of wealth. The Irakun of Tanzania wear decorative raffia skirts as an indication of refined elegance. The *jocolo* is worn for the first time by newly married Ndebele women in South Africa, symbolising their new status in society. The *kilimtrabersi* or «Kilim de Tripoli» is in Berber tradition, a strong element of continuity and geographical identification. This cloth was brought by native Berbers from Libya who had immigrated almost a century earlier into Tunisia and had been called "those who created Egyptian fashion" by the Khiymiya. The language of traditional signs, beliefs or skills such as the making of flat-woven mats known as Kilims is the origin of ancient cultural stories reinforced by superstition and passed on from mother to daughter. The need of registering the continuity for the wealth accumulated and the fertility as well as the ownership of the land is the basis of a visual form of communication which could be carried from one place to another: Kilims were the result[61]. Following the six directions of the Berber universe, the "Land of the setting sun" also known as Maghreb was invaded and settled by Arabs between 670 and 700 CE. The Kilim tradition was found among the 600 registered tribes of Berbers in Morocco (the only North African country which was never part of the Ottoman Empire). Among these Berbers, kilims woven by the Zemmour are among the most popular among the weaving tribes on the coast of Morocco. The signs used by the Zemmour are mainly triangles, crosses, zigzag and diamond shapes in orange, white, black, green and yellow. The materials used are cotton, silk and wool despite the modern use of synthetics. *Kente* was for centuries the textile reserved for the royal family of the *Asantehene*, the king of Ashanti in Ghana, but it is now mass produced and symbolises the independence of the continent. The artist El Anatsui has shown in his major work, « Kente Rhapsody », the changes and ill-effects of

---

61. *Kilim, the Complete Guide* by Alastair Hull & Jose Luczyc-Wyhowska (Chronicle Books 2000)

the commercialization of this traditional cloth which has damaged its traditional use. In conclusion, the effect of Western culture on modern African applied art is to distort it to conform with the Western point of view. They want Western ideas of beauty and their desire for fashion makes them forget the culture and history represented by their own style of dress. The world of cosmetics which we have analysed in these pages bears witness to this situation, one where a cultural heritage has had to transform itself to answer the needs of an African population evolving for several generations in a foreign land without knowing or understanding their original culture and its codes of adornment.

Textile language among the Somali people before the war (1991) was originally similar between men and women. In order to better understand the dress history of the Somali people, it is interesting to go back to their history. From 1888 until 1960 the Somali people were colonised by Italy (Somalia) and Britain (Somaliland) with parts ruled by France (now Djibouti) and Ethiopia. Heather Marie Akou[62] divides the fashion history of the Somalis into three distinctive periods: before colonization; between 1888 and 1945, the main period of colonisation, and from 1945 to 1991, from the end of Italian rule and after independence in 1960. We will mainly focus on the period starting in 1945 as the dress codes have dramatically changed during that period due to several socio-economic factors. The first factor was the education of young Somali men outside the country - in Europe and the Middle East. On their return home, they would influence the lifestyle which was half traditional and half a consequence of the presence of Europeans, Arabs and Asians. Somali society contains castes and classes and the dress code was a way of classifying people. The colonial experience added an extra code of appearance: facial features. Somali people who looked Asian or European had a better social presence than those who looked "African" in their physical appearance. As a consequence, the lighter the skin, the straighter the nose and hair, the more easily they would be publicly accepted. Furthermore, the bloodline

---

62. *The Politics of Dress in Somali Culture*, Heather Marie Akou (Indiana University Press 2011).

was as equally significant: slaves' descendants for example could be seen wearing nose rings which was unacceptable among the descendants of dominant families. On the other hand, hair bleaching was a practice spread among the nomadic Somali, never seen among the rich Somali rich traders and the intellectuals. The people who travelled and studied abroad had "to create" fashion and to readapt to their initial environment. As they felt they had gained extra skills and been exposed to other standards of living and dress codes, they wanted to acknowledge this part of their life journeys by wearing European or Arab style clothes. This social change also allowed those born into less privileged families and backgrounds to emancipate themselves from the traditional Somali class system. As colonization ended, these classes of intellectuals together with the rich Somali local traders and the army were the people who were left to run the country. While a vast majority of inhabitants was still wearing Somali cotton and leather outfits, these upper classes were recognized through their opportunities to trade or interact with foreigners. In a word, the post-colonial Somali upper class was the new Somali establishment. Soon a dress code policy based on Western dress would be laid down following the arrival in the government of intellectuals supported by and supporting an orthodox application of Islam. Shortly after the official decolonization process ended and Europeans left Somalia, the Somali government of of the late 1960s and 1970s which associated Europeanized clothes with colonialism, banned both the traditional and the Westernized outfits from the streets in towns and cities.

Leather was the principal material used by nomadic Somali as cattle was the primary source of income: food, clothes, secondary uses of bones and greases were valuable. A piece of leather was often knotted over one shoulder leaving both arms, lower legs and shoulders uncovered to allow body flexibility. As mainly nomadic people, most of their styling attention was focused on the whiteness of their teeth and the cleanliness of their hair.

PART IV: TEXTILES: BODY ADORNMENT   — 4) COLOURS AND ADORNMENT THROUGH COLOURS.

92

b) The Use of Textiles

The Bafia people in the Mbam region of Cameroon, because of the climate and context where they lived wore few clothes in the case of men and protective clothes in the case of women. The skin was oiled with various oils and adorned with accessories handed down from the family ancestry with spiritual and symbolic value. Clothing was more a spiritual act than a physical necessity. In "being clothed" people were thinking about being "spiritually armed" to defend its own life within the different spiritual spheres (see the first chapter dedicated to Bantu cosmogony). According to Margaret Trowell[63], ".....Proverbs, allegories, adages and wise words form the backcloth to African thought, and both the myths and legends of the tribal past and the prestige of the reigning chief or king are summed up in aphorisms or visual symbols ...." In other words, ancient Africans were mapping their identities using textiles and eventually beadwork to record a designed or picture version of a story, an event or a sacred message. Knowing that in ancient Egypt, jewellery was sometimes used as part of a dress code, being used for the broad "collars" so typically found on most pictures of that period[64]. Mainly made of rows of pendants and beads in turquoise, green or red, these "collars" could also be made of cheaper stones for the lower social classes including amethyst, garnet or jasper. Gold was always the privilege of royal families. People in ancient Egypt took their designs from nature and adapted them to decorate their accessories. Beadwork which is an important art form in modern east, west and southern Africa is still associated with status: chiefs and sacred objects are adorned symbolically with a local significance. Hatshepsut, one of the few female pharaohs of ancient Egypt who have ruled from 1479 to 1458 BCE during the 18th dynasty; was known for her penchant for wearing pharaoh's attire including the royal head cloth and the false beard as accessories. Her mortuary temple is situated in modern Deil El Bahri (Valley of the Kings). Hatshepsut was one

---

63. *African Design* by Margaret Trowell (Faber & Faber1960)

64. *Ancient Egyptian Designs* by Eva Wilson (British Museum Pattern books 1986)

of the few pharaohs who extensively built temples and obelisks as a remembrance of her reign. Grand-daughter of Ahmose who himself fought the Hyksos and installed the "Valley of the Kings", the "She-King of Egypt"[65] was buried without accessories or gold, as royals were all supposed to. Ornaments as symbol of power in ancient African cultures were widespread as customs and as a means of social recognition and identification in life and on the death bed. Perceived as adornments which could be similar to clothing, ornaments made of jewels were highly regarded as a sign of distinction. According to a description of people in Congo in 1591 their clothes were "garments made from the palm tree of beautiful craftsmanship..."[66]. Fibres such as raffia and screw-pine were commonly used in the traditional weaving techniques to create clothes and textiles. Raffia was traditionally coloured using vegetable dye in red/yellow, ochre, lavender and black. Cotton and silk were more often seen (and still are) in the ancient kingdom of Dahomey (now Benin) and in modern Nigeria.

65. Named by Chip Brown in National Geographic April 2009 page 88 and cover

66. *History of the kingdom of Congo* by Duante Lopez (1591) translated by Filippo Pigafetta

PART V: ACCESSORIZING THE BODY

1) ANCIENT AFRICA

a) The Mangbetu

Beautifying the body is also about ornaments and accessories. In this last part modern West Africa, Hamitic (Somali) and Sudanese cultures from Central Africa (Mangbetu) will served as basis to introduce the ancient and modern codes of aesthetics in Africa. Chosen because of their particularities and precision in their social contexts, these parts of Africa are among a more global and codified ways of adorning the bodies using materials others than clothes or paints. These accessories are worn sometimes as hair jewels by male, female and sometimes children as strict codes of collective recognition.

The Mangbetu probably originated from what is now South Sudan and settled in the north east of the modern Democratic Republic of Congo (DRC). Their secluded kingdoms were first visited by the German explorer Georg Schweinfurth in 1870. They were known for their pride in wearing jewellery made out of ivory and for adorning their hair with hairpins and their bodies with anklets. Collars and bracelets had a deep significance for the wearer. Artistic ornamentation of any kind – on the body, on furniture or on their houses – was a privilege only for the ruling classes. Who were exclusively from a Mangbetu bloodline despite the fact that many of the people living on their lands (which they occupied in the 18th and 19th centuries) were of other ethnic groups

Beautifully designed jewellery in many different shapes and using a variety of materials was used to decorate belts, hats, hairpins and bracelets. Finely carved ivory decorated with with copper, iron or glass (introduced by European traders) were highly sought after by the Mangbetu elite. These ornaments were even more important for the daily beautification for the Mangbetu people than their other practices: scarification, *lopombo*, the art of stretching the head or neck, and body painting. The picture of Queen Mutubani of the Mangbetu illustrates this (circa 1910).[67]

b) The Somali

Among the Somali, as for the Mangbetu, wealth was more likely to be measured by the bloodline and size of the land belonging to the family. Jewellery also had an important value. According to their original beliefs, amulets were cherished among most social classes as they protected people from evil spirits and prevented bad behaviour within the community. The Somali art of accessorizing had different historical phases and periods (see preceding section). Known as Hamitic people with a Cushitic culture and system of value, the Somali people are mainly present in modern Somalia (including Somaliland), Djibouti and parts of Kenya and Ethiopia. While the Somali seem to trace back their origins to a brotherhood: Samaal and Saab. Six distinctive clans

---

67. Source: *Mangbetu Pottery: Tradition and Innovation in Northeast Zaire.* Enid Schildkrout, Jill Hellman and Curtis A.Keim. African Arts 22 (2):38-47. http://diglib1.amnh.org/articles/anthro/excerpt2.html

compose a majority of the Somali population, divided into two main groups: the Samaal include the Digil and the Rahanweyn both culturally semi- nomadic; the Saab include the Darod, the Dir, the Hawiyah and the Isaaq, mainly sedentary farmers who have assimilated some of the Asian and Arab cultural influences brought by centuries of trading with these parts of the world. To these two groups can be added the Boni who are supposedly the original inhabitants of the land; the Habasho (also subdivided into smaller groups) who are perceived as descendants of former slaves; the Bajun who are of Asian descent; the Eile, survivors of an ancient population; and the Amarani, related to Bantu-speaking Africans. This variety will allow a better appreciation of the particularities and differences within Somali culture.

Habits and lifestyles were different in the nomadic and sedentary traditions. The Saab who owned land started buying materials imported from other parts of the world to indicate their wealth and social status and distinguished themselves from the other Somali cultures. Despite the fact that they all shared the same hairstyles, abandoned the traditional dress (leather and accessories), the jewellery they used was distinctive in terms of gender, occupation and wealth. The *audulli,* an expensive necklace made of silver, amber and other beads, was symbolically worn by well-off women who had husbands wealthy enough to trade with international partners. On the other hand, wearing jewellery on the nose could have been perceived as a practice of the Habasho people, descended from slaves, which was despised. Jewels had to be worn on certain parts of the body in association with certain materials. Similarly, the Samaal were known to constantly wear their "amulets" everywhere and anywhere as protective items, symbolically showing that they belonged to a nomadic clan. Both men and women wore these amulets which, for the wealthy, were sometimes made of amber and often decorated with words from the Qu'ran.

c) West Africa

The art of adorning the body in some other parts of the continent are correlated to the power of life forces: fertility, femininity and life itself. The most widespread type of sexually significant accessory used to create the best environment in which to conceive a child is the of wearing of *jaljali* , beads which are often worn around the waist and sometimes around the breasts. Cowries are used, sometimes together with rare and precious materials. The wearing of many beads is recommended and popular as it symbolizes the number of potential children. The *jaljali* are supposed to protect the women's fertility and eventually increase it which is why they have to be worn around a woman's waist. During the day the *jaljali* is worn as an adornment but it can also mean that the woman is looking forward to getting pregnant or in the evening or at night it can help increase her femininity and encourage sexual intercourse with her husband. Femininity is not considered to be separate from motherhood and to have given birth is the sign of a truly fulfilled women. Childbearing is central to the cultures of West Africa and the tradition of wearing beads around the waist is widespread in most of the countries in the region.

2) ABOUT BODY HEADWRAPPING

Head and body wrapping started in the time of the ancient Egyptians who developed the practice to the highest levels of both aesthetics and hygiene. There are different methods of wrapping both the body and head which are still current today in Africa and the Diaspora. As discussed in the previous part, body wrapping in Africa was influenced by the hot climate, by the migration of peoples and by the availability of textiles. Depending where people were living wrapping the body would be one option to facilitate movement, or in other conditions body painting would be favoured. In all cases, members of royal families wore textiles wrapped around their bodies. We will focus on head wrapping among women as this is still a widespread practice. According to the Book of the Dead, wrapping was primarily to protect and preserve the body for a better travel to the afterlife. Bandaging the deceased person was both a ceremonial and a highly skilled process lasting up to two weeks. Wrapping the body was performed to keep all the parts of the body together, to preserve the body moistures for the long journey into the afterlife and finally to give the body a final shape to fit the sarcophagus. The methods and quality of material used help modern Egyptologists to date and classify the different types of mummies.

Anubis observing a wrapped body.

In Ivory Coast, head wrapping was mainly used for married women to indicate their geographical origin. Similarly the Yoruba *gele* attracts the eye to the wearer while also confirming her marital status. Originally supposed to cover the entire hair line, head wrapping is common today in West and Central Africa and it encourages a focus on womens' facial features. As always, the dress code allows people within the community to understand the social significance without having to ask.

One of the best examples of this tradition is the well-defined and codified practice of head wrapping in Martinique. Six types of head wrapping also called *Maré Tèt* were broadly used among Afro-Caribbean women of Martinique. As in the time of slavery, wearing hats was forbidden for black slaves according to the highly disputed *Code Noir*[68]: only freed blacks could eventually own a piece of land or marry whomever they wanted to. Before the Code Noir laws were changed in 1724, any parent who was free could allow his child to inherit his status. After 1724 new Code Noir laws restricted the principles and applications of slave emancipation by birth and the bad treatment of slaves brought from the coast of Africa led a high death rate among them and fewer births. More mixed race children were born at this time. As a result, children could only inherit the status of the mother: the child of a freed mother would be freed. Born to a slave mother, the child would remain a slave. A freed father would have to recognize the child, baptise the child and "buy" the child to make him or her free. Technically children born as a result of rape were slaves unless the slave owning father agreed to free them between the age of 15 to 20. Consequently, female African slaves quickly understood that marriage or sexual relations with whites could open the door to emancipation. Acknowledging their marital status and condition became vital: codified head wrapping was born. In their Creole languages, names were given such as: the "Moussor" - the original style from which only the ends of the head wrap can be modified to design a certain shape: the "Eventail", "Marie-Claire", "Plume de Carpot", the " Plume de Blaise Diagne" the "Signara" and the "Teleli" depending on the number of ends.

68. Legal texts "regulating" African slave trade and code of conduct in French West Indies (Guadeloupe, Guyane, Saint Domingue (Haiti), Martinique and la Réunion) applied from March 1685 to March 1848 but were modified in 1724,

Illustration: No. 1 and 3, woman wearing one visible end: "Chaumière"
or "Tête à 1 bout" (a woman is free from any relationship).

No.2, woman wearing 3 visible ends: "Tête à 3 bouts" (married woman
deeply in love with her husband).

No. 4, woman wearing 2 visible ends: "Tête à 2 bouts" (engaged woman
but available to other men).

No. 5, women wearing 4 visible ends: Tête à 4 bouts"(in a relationship
but available to other men)

Several styles which were created at that time are still maintained today
to acknowledge a woman's status during festivals and carnivals.

CONCLUSION

Body adornment in Africa is a wide concept, an art form providing personal identification through the quest for beautification. It bears testimony to cultural, sociology and economic history. Different trends of painting, scarifying, styling hair and dressing the body with clothes and ornaments have been developing for thousands of years, taking into account varied geographical backgrounds and social realities. The symbolism of colours to manifest and differentiate individuals, the use of body painting for sacred or hidden messages, tattooing for spiritual protection, dressing to establish status, all these ingredients form the core of highly codified institutions. Controversial practices such as extreme body modification including FGM and breast ironing find their roots in a shift of cultural patterns. Initially with a social meaning, these practices have become over-used protective methods of controlling of the body: they are not cultural, social or religious commandments but interpretations of how to take control over people's bodies. Possessing one's body by mapping it and locking it into a particular way of thinking is a reminder of long traditions of marking corpses with encoded identities, using the flesh as final way of communicating. African beauty practices are horizontal[69] forms of communication apart from being both visual and tactile so as to share an idea of beauty where this beauty represents distinctiveness. African body adornment shows continuity with practices found as far away as the West Indies and the United States: hair braiding, skin caring using oils to massage the dermis and the popularity of textile wrapping as a manageable way to dress heads and bodies, all these are reminders of a long African history.

THE END

---

69. Horizontal communication is the ability to communicate between people at the same level in a given organization. Horizontal communication strategy aims at developing teamwork.

BIBLIOGRAPHY

Adler, P. & Bernard N. *African majesty, the textile art of the Ashante and Ewe* (Thames and Hudson 1992)

Akou, Heather M. *The Politics of Dress in Somali Culture* (Indiana University Press 2011)

Arnoldi, M.J and Kreamer, C. M. *Crossing Achievements, African Art of Dressing the Head,* (Article in Journal of Asian and African Studies1995)

Ashton, Sally-A. *Origins of Afro comb* (Cambridge, Fitzwilliam Museum exhibition 2012)

Austermann, U. E. E. *A compendium of cosmetology & aesthetics.* (Nelson Thornes, reprint 1987)

Bacquard, J.B. *The Tribal Arts of Africa* (Thames and Hudson 2004)

Bailey, Diane C. *Natural Hair Care & Braiding* (Milady 1998)

Barker-Benfield, G. J. *The Horror of the Half-Known Life* (Broadway 1976)

Bedwith, C. & Fisher, A. *Painted Bodies: African Body Painting, Tattoos, and Scarification* (Rizzoli International 2012)

Begoun, P. *Don't Go to the Cosmetics Counter Without Me* (Beginning Press2009)

Bourdieu, P. *Distinction* (Harvard University Press 1984)

Breward, C. *Fashion* .(Oxford History of Art, OUP Oxford 2003)Bundles, A'Lelia. *On her own Ground* (Scribner 2002)

Browne, G. Afro Hair - Procedures and Techniques(Hyperion Books 1989)

Bundles, A'Lelia *Madam C. J. Walker: Entrepreneur* (Chelsea House/Facts on File, 2008)

Bundles, A'Lelia *On Her Own Ground: The Life and Times of Madam C.J. Walker* (Lisa Drew Books/Scribner, 2001)

Bush, B. *Slave Women in Caribbean Society 1650-1838* (Heinemann, 1990)

Byrd, A. D. & Tharps, L. L. *Hair history: untangling the roots of black hair in America* (St. Martin's Griffin 2002)

Clark, Leon E. *Through African Eyes, Vol 1. The past: Road to Independence* (CITE Books 1999)

Cooper, J.C *An Illustrated Encyclopaedia of Traditional Symbols* (Thames & Hudson 1978).

Corson, R. *Fashion in Make-up ,from Ancient to Modern Times* (Peter Owen1972).

Corson, R. *Fashion in Hair* (Peter Owen 1965)

Cressy, S. *Illustrated Beauty Therapy Dictionary* (Heinemann 2008)

de Marees, Pieter, van Dantzig, (Tr. A., Jones, A.) *Description & historical account of the gold kingdom of Guinea 1602.* (Oxford University Press for the British Academy 1987)

De Mello, M. *Encyclopedia of Body Adornment.*(Greenwood Press2007)

Diop, Cheikh A. *The African Origin of Civilization: Myth or Reality*(A Cappella Books 1974)

Diop, Cheikh A. *Civilization or Barbarism* (Lawrence Hill Books1960)

Ebong, I. & Bundles, A. *Black hair: Art, Style and Culture* (Universe 2001)

Eltayeb, A. *1991 Demographic & Heath Survey* (Republic of Sudan)

Fanon, F. *Black Skin, White Masks*(Pluto Press 1986)

Fairley, J. *The Ultimate Natural Beauty Book* (Kyle Cathie 2004)

Ford, G. *Hairdressing with Barbering & African Hair Type Hair Units* (Harlow-Heinemann 2009).

Geoffroy-Schneiter, B. *Ethnic style, history and fashion* (2002).

Gimbel, T. *Colour Therapy Workbook* (Thorsons 2002).

Hart, R. *Plantation society: a Study of the Sugar Plantation in the Caribbean* (1996).

Hatton, P. *Afro hair, a salon handbook.*(Blackwell Scientific 1994)

Hawthorne, S. *Wild politics: feminism, globalisation, bio-diversity* (Spinifex Press (2002).

Hiscock, J. and others *Illustrated hairdressing dictionary.* Pearson Education (2008)

Howse, C. *Ultra Black Hair Growth 2* (UBH publications 2001)

Hull, A. & Luczyc-Wyhowska, J. *Kilim : The Complete Guide: History, Pattern, Technique, Identification* (Chronicle Books 2000).

Kechara, S., *The Ultimate Beauty Book: over 100 Natural Recipes for Gorgeous Healthy Skin*. (Greenbooks 2008)

Kenner, T. A., *Symbols and their hidden meanings* (Carlton Books2006)

Klem, O. Amelia, *The Tattooed Lady*, (Speck Press 2009)

Lanji, R. *"Enamoured"* exhibition in London Revlon 2012)

Lilly, S. *Modern Colour Therapy* (Caxton Publishing 2002)

Lister, Maurice *Men's hairdressing, traditional and modern barbering*(Thomson2004)

Miller,J.C The Body Art (Berkley Publishing Corporation 1997)

Mistlin, I. *How to win Clients and interpret their needs.*(Blackwell Scientific Publications1994)

Modest, W. *The Body Adorned* **Horniman Museum exhibition2012)**

Morrow, Willie L. *400 Years without a Comb* (Black Publishers1973)

Murray, S. & Roscoe W. *Boy-Wives and Female Husbands: Studies in African*

Homosexualities (St.Martins Press 1998)

Nelson M. *Make your own Make-up* (Sixth & Spring Books 2005)

Obenga, T. *Les Bantu, Langues-Peuples-Civilisations*, (Transaction1989).

Openshaw, F. *Hairdressing Science* (Longman1982)

Persadsingh, Dr. N. *The Hair in Black Women* (2002)

Picton, J. & Mack, J. *African textiles* (Harper & Row 1989)

Pitts, V. *In the flesh*. Palgrave Macmillan (2003)

Reiger, Martin M. *Harry's Cosmeticology, Volumes I-II, 8th Edition)* Chemical Publishing Company 2000)

Rosenthal, S. *Women and Unwanted Hair* . (Your Health Press 2001)

Rounce, J. *Science for the beauty therapist* (Nelson Thornes1983)

Sagay, E. *African hairstyles, styles of yesterday and today*. (Heinemann Educational Books1983)

Saulnier, P. *Plantes médicinales et soins en Afrique*, (Saint-Maur 1998)

Shepherd, R &R*1000 symbols*. (Thames &Hudson 2002)

Spring, C. & Hudson, J. *Silk in Africa*.(British Museum 2002)

Schoon, D. *Nail structure and product chemistry.*(Milady 2005)

Sherrow, V. *Encyclopaedia of Hair, a Cultural History* (Greenwood Publishing Group 2006)

Sieber, R. & Herreman, F. *Hair in African art and culture* (Prestel 2000)

Standish J. *How not to wear Black* (O Books 2011)

Stavert E. *Beauty Masks and Scrubs* (Guild of Master Craftsman Publications 2010)

Steele, V. *Encyclopaedia of clothing and fashion, volume 1*(Scribner Publication 2005)

Trowell, M. *African Design*(Faber& Faber 1960)

Thomas D. *Soulstyle: Black Women redefining the Color of Fashion* (Harper Collins 1987)

Udale, J. *Basics fashion design (02): textiles & fashion* (AVA Publishing 2008)

Vaughan-Richards A. *Black and Beautiful* (Longman International 1986)

Wilkinson, Sir J.G. *Manners and Customs of the Ancient Egyptians* (publ. 1837)

Willett, F. *African Art* (Thames and Hudson World of Art series 2002)

Wilson, E. *Ancient Egyptian Designs* (British Museum Pattern Books, British Museum Press1986)

Web contacts:

http://www.euromonitor.com/

http://www.forwarduk.org.uk/

http://www.habia.org/c/1797/standards

http://www.haircouncil.org.uk/

The New York Times "Wealthiest Negress Dead May 26th 1919", www.nytimes.

com/learning/general/onthisday/bday/1223.html

http://www.worldofbraidingacademy.com

Films and documentaries:

Kimbell R. (2006-2008) My Nappy Roots a journey through Black Hair-itage educational version documentary, Virgin MOON entertainment

Articles in Magazines:

Arise Magazine (January 2013), interviewing Waris Dirie

Euromonitor International, article on 14 September 2012 "Ethnic Beauty Care poised for a New Area of Growth" by Rob Walker

Euromonitor International, article on 29 October 2012 "Men's Grooming on the Cusp of Transformation" by

Nicole Tyrimou

National Geographic (February 2008), Photographs of Nubian pharaohs by Kenneth Garrett

National Geographic (April 2009) "The She-King of Egypt" by Chip Brown

GLOSSARY

Argan – oil-baring seed from the argan tree

Berbers – the main indigenous people of north Africa

Bissap – hibiscus tea, also juice from its bark, used as a drink in west Africa

Caucasian – generic name for the "white" races

Cinnamaldehyde - a viscous liquid found in the bark of the cinnamon tree

Cortex – the outer layer of certain organs

Cuticle – outermost skin or dead skin

Dermis – skin below the outer layer

Epidermis – cuticle or external skin

Ester – a compound formed by her condensation of an alcohol and an acid, without water

Galenite – lead sulphate, lead ore

Kemet – the ancient Egyptian name for Egypt

keratin – the essential ingredient of nails, horns etc.

khôl - a mineral powder made of lead, sulphur and animal fat

Maghreb – north western Africa

Medullary area – inner portion of hair or tissue

Natron – a hydrated carbonate of sodium found on some lake shores

Oligo elements –small quantities of nutrients or mineral elements necessary for life

Papilla- small protuberance or elevation of the skin

Papyrus – paper made from reeds used in ancient Egypt

Saponins – a class of chemical compounds producing a soapy substance

Sebaceous – relating to the fatty secretion that lubricates the hair

Sumerians – the ancient civilised people of Mesopotamia (modern Iraq)

Tuareg – nomadic ethnic group living in the Sahara

Index

H

Habasho 97
HABIA (the Hair and Beauty
　　Industry Authority) 34
Hairstyling 25, 26
Hanafites 73
Hanbalites 73
Hathor 66, 89
Hawiyah 97
Heather Marie Akou 91
HyKsos 25

I

Indo-European communities 35
Irakun of Tanzania 90
Isaaq 97
Isis 78, 81, 85
Ivory Coast 44, 99

J

jaljali 98
Jean-Chris Miller 69

K

Kaleri 67
Karo 66
Kemet 25, 31, 32, 83, 110
Khoisan 48
kilimtrabersi or « Kilim de Tripoli
　　90
Kirdi 68
Krishna 77
Virender Kumar 77

L

Maurice Lister 37
LiyaKebede 38
Lobi 68

M

Macy Gray 38
Maghreb 89, 90, 110

Miriam Makeba 43
makruma 73
Makruma 73
Malikites 73
Mangbetu 95, 96
Pieter de Marees 26
Margo DeMello 66, 70
Rita Marley 43
Martinique 18, 20, 99, 100
Masai 43
Mbam 71, 93
Mediterranean 16
Menes 31
Missy Elliott 38
Willie L. Morrow 19
Mursi 66, 68

N

Narmer 31
negroid 17
Neti 78
New York 23, 24, 42, 43
Nigeria 50, 67, 94
North Africa 26, 65
Nuba 67
Nubia 12
Nubian hair 20
Nut 78
Nuwaupu 31, 32

O

Olympus 80
Osiris 78, 84, 85
Ottoman Turks 26

P

Pakistan 77
Peckham 43
Pharaoh 23
Pierre 25, 65
Pierre Bourdieu 25
Prince Albert 87
Ptah 16